AS/A-LEVEL YEAR 1

STUDENT GUIDE

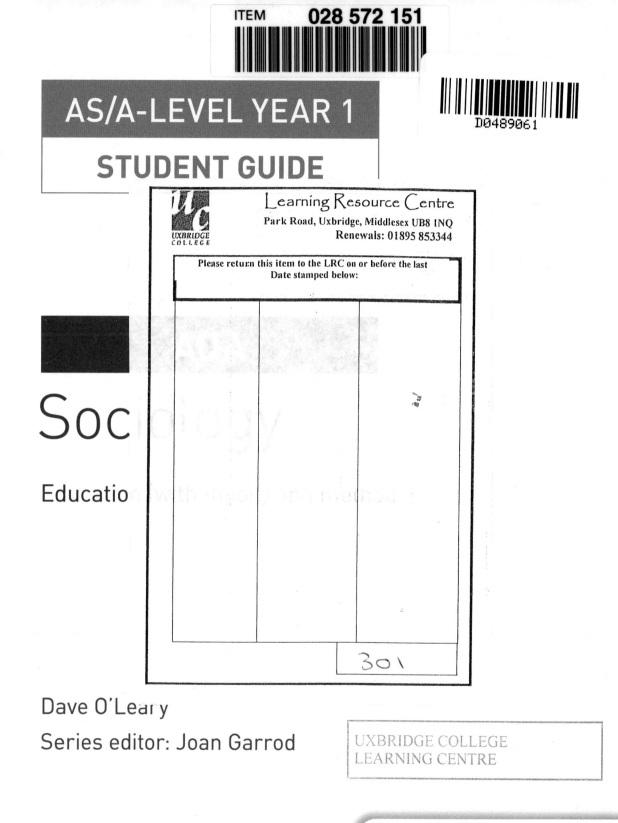

Sociology

Education with theory and methods

Dave O'Leary

Series editor: Joan Garrod

PHILIP ALLAN FOR
HODDER
EDUCATION
AN HACHETTE UK COMPANY

Acknowledgement: the author would like to thank the sociology students at Kingsthorpe College for their support.

Philip Allan, an imprint of Hodder Education, an Hachette UK company, Blenheim Court, George Street, Banbury, Oxfordshire OX16 5BH

Orders

Bookpoint Ltd, 130 Park Drive, Milton Park, Abingdon, Oxfordshire OX14 4SB

tel: 01235 827827

fax: 01235 400401

e-mail: education@bookpoint.co.uk

Lines are open 9.00 a.m.–5.00 p.m., Monday to Saturday, with a 24-hour message answering service. You can also order through the Hodder Education website: www.hoddereducation.co.uk

ISBN 978-1-4718-4432-4

First printed 2015

Impression number 5 4 3 2 1

Year 2019 2018 2017 2016 2015

This Guide has been written specifically to support students preparing for the AQA AS and A-level Sociology examinations. The content has been neither approved nor endorsed by AQA and remains the sole responsibility of the author.

Typeset by Integra Software Services Pvt. Ltd., Pondicherry, India

Cover photo: Marco Govel/Fotolia

Printed in Italy

Hachette UK's policy is to use papers that are natural, renewable and recyclable products and made from wood grown in sustainable forests. The logging and manufacturing processes are expected to conform to the environmental regulations of the country of origin.

Contents

Content Guidance

Questions & Answers

■ Getting the most from this book

Exam tips

Advice on key points in the text to help you learn and recall content, avoid pitfalls, and polish your exam technique in order to boost your grade.

Knowledge check

Rapid-fire questions throughout the Content Guidance section to check your understanding.

Knowledge check answers

1 Turn to the back of the book for the Knowledge check answers.

Summaries

- Each core topic is rounded off by a bullet-list summary for quick-check reference of what you need to know.

Exam-style questions

Commentary on the questions

Tips on what you need to do to gain full marks, indicated by the icon **e**

Sample student answers

Practise the questions, then look at the student answers that follow.

Questions & Answers

■ Test paper 2

AS Paper 2 (Section A): Research methods

(01) Outline two problems of using laboratory experiments in sociological research. (4 marks)

e Make sure you refer to specific problems of laboratory experiments and not field experiments.

(02) Evaluate the problems of using overt participant observation in sociological research. (16 marks)

e Use Template 1 for methods questions on page 45. Make sure you focus on overt PO and only use other types of observation for comparative analysis and evaluation.

Student A

01 ■ Hawthorne effect, as if people know they are being observed their behaviour may change.
■ They lack ecological validity as they take place in an artificial environment.
■ They may cause both physical and mental harm to the participants.

e 4/4 marks awarded. All three responses are correct. It is a good strategy to use bullet points and give an extra example just in case one of the first two is incorrect.

02 Overt participant observation (OPO) is a form of observation in which the researcher makes their true identity and purpose known. OPO is favoured by interpretivists as it provides a valid, first-hand insight as the researcher is actually joining in with the activities of those being studied. However, positivists reject the use of OPO due to its lack of reliability, generalisability and representativeness. Positivists would prefer to use overt non-participant observation as this would more easily allow the researcher to use a structured observation schedule which could be used to gain reliable data due to its standardised nature.

e Good use of WWWE as outlined in Template 1 and good comparison with non-participant observation.

One of the practical issues of OPO is 'getting in'. Groups such as criminal gangs would be unlikely to allow a researcher access to study them as they may see them as the 'police in disguise'. An example of this is Patrick, who

Commentary on sample student answers

Find out how many marks each answer would be awarded in the exam and then read the comments (preceded by the icon **e**) following each student answer.

■ About this book

This guide is for students following the AQA AS and A-level Sociology courses. It deals with the topics of education and sociological theory and methods. At AS these are examined in Paper 1 Education with methods in context and Paper 2 (Section A) Research methods. At A-level they are examined in Paper 1 Education with theory and methods.

There are two main sections to this guide.

■ **Content Guidance** — this provides details of the topics of education and sociological theory and methods. Topic areas on education and theory and methods examine **key ideas** and arguments, stating the main points of evaluation and listing the **key concepts** and **key thinkers**. The defined words are key words for this specification.

■ **Questions and Answers** — this shows you the kind of questions you can expect in the AS Paper 1 and Paper 2 Section A examinations and in the A-level Paper 1 examination. The first three test papers are followed by two sample answers: Candidate A (A-grade response) and Candidate B (C-grade response). The fourth test paper has practice AS and A-level papers for you to attempt yourself with guidance on how to answer.

How to use this guide

When you study education topics and theory and methods in class, read the corresponding information from the Content Guidance section to become familiar with the topic. You should use this information to complete your own revision notes, for example on each method and topic within education. If you are doing the AS exam, you can complete Test Paper 1 practice exam questions after completing the education topic and Test Paper 2 when you have finished the methods topic. You will need to complete the question on methods in context after you have finished both topics. It is advisable to focus on one essay question at a time. After you have completed your own answers you should compare them with the answers from Candidates A and B. These and the commentary can be used to amend your revision notes. If you are doing the A-level exam, you can go through the same process with Test Paper 3. While Test Paper 3 has A-level exam questions, question 05 is in the same format as the Methods in Context question in AS Paper 1 and so will also be useful when revising for this exam.

The AS and A-level specifications are shown in detail on the AQA website: www.aqa.org.uk/7912. Follow the links to Sociology AS (7191) and A-level (7192).

Content Guidance

This section outlines the major issues and themes of **Education** and **Sociological theory and methods**. Note that **theory** is required for A-level only.

The content of **Education** (AS and A-level) falls into the following areas:
- The role and functions of the education system, including its relationship to the economy and to class structure
- Differential educational achievement of social groups by social class, gender and ethnicity in contemporary society
- Relationships and processes within schools, with particular reference to teacher/ pupil relationships, pupil identities and subcultures, the hidden curriculum, and the organisation of teaching and learning
- The significance of educational policies, including policies of selection, marketisation and privatisation, and policies to achieve greater equality of opportunity or outcome, for an understanding of the structure, role, impact and experience of and access to education; the impact of globalisation on educational policy

The content of **Sociological methods** (AS and A-level) falls into following areas:
- Quantitative and qualitative methods of research; research design
- Sources of data, including questionnaires, interviews, participant and non-participant observation, experiments, documents and official statistics
- The distinction between primary and secondary data, and between quantitative and qualitative data
- The relationship between positivism, interpretivism and sociological methods; the nature of 'social facts'
- The theoretical, practical and ethical considerations influencing choice of topic, choice of method(s) and the conduct of research

The content of **Sociological theory** (A-level only) falls into following areas:
- Consensus, conflict, structural and social action theories
- The concepts of modernity and postmodernity in relation to sociological theory
- The nature of science and the extent to which sociology can be regarded as scientific
- The relationship between theory and methods
- Debates about subjectivity, objectivity and value freedom
- The relationship between sociology and social policy

For both AS and A-level you will be required to apply the information from sociological research methods to the study of education in the **Methods in context** question (see page 48 for specific guidance on this question).

■ The role and functions of education

Functionalism

Key ideas

Functionalists see the role of the education system as positive for both the individual and society. They argue that it has three main functions: socialisation, economic and selection (SES).

Socialisation

- **Durkheim** (1903) argued that education promoted **social solidarity** through creating shared values. Things such as teaching a common history and having assemblies would help bind students together and help create a **value consensus**.
- **Parsons** (1961) argued that education acted as a bridge between the **particularistic** values of the home and the **universalistic** values of society. He felt education was crucial in secondary socialisation and had become the **focal socialising agency**.

Economic

- Durkheim felt that the role of education was not only to provide general values but also specific skills (such as numeracy and literacy) needed for the world of work.
- Parsons argued that education socialises young people to believe that society is **meritocratic**. This prepares them for the individualistic and competitive nature of the economy.

Selection

- **Davis and Moore** (1945) argued that the education system helps to **'sift and sort'** people into the most appropriate position in the economy (**role allocation**).

Value consensus When there is agreement on key principles and norms in society.

Meritocratic A meritocracy is when social rewards are based on effort and ability rather than being born into a position. Equal opportunities help ensure status is achieved, not ascribed.

Evaluation

- + Education does perform a key role in secondary socialisation and acts as a bridge between the family and wider society.
- + Education does have an important role in skills provision and allocating future work roles.
- − Marxists have a different view on the three functions:
  - ■ Socialisation. Rather than shared values education transmits ruling-class ideology.
  - ■ Economic. Education reproduces docile, obedient workers for capitalism.
  - ■ Selection. Meritocracy is a myth and the education system legitimates inequality.
- − Interactionists argue that functionalists ignore 'micro' processes in schools.
- − Feminists argue that **patriarchy** within education is ignored. There are not equal opportunities for females in education.

Patriarchy The dominance of men over women.

Key concepts

secondary socialisation; social solidarity; value consensus; meritocracy; role allocation

Key thinkers

Durkheim, Parsons, Davis and Moore

Marxism

Key ideas

- **Althusser** argues that education is an **ideological state apparatus** (ISA), a tool used by capitalism to make society seem fair. He argues that education **legitimates** inequality by making it seem that failure is down to the individual rather than being the fault of the school.
- Althusser also argues that the education system **reproduces** class inequality as working-class pupils end up in the same type of job as their parents.
- **Bowles and Gintis** similarly argue that the **myth of meritocracy** ensures that the working class blame themselves for their failure at school, therefore legitimising class inequality. They argue that there is a **correspondence principle** as school mirrors work — for example, they are both based on hierarchy, rewards, obedience and set routines.
- The **hidden curriculum** (the 'untaught' lessons such as punctuality and punishments for not doing homework) prepares working-class pupils to accept their low position in the capitalist economy.
- **Bourdieu** argues that the education system leads to **cultural reproduction**. Rather than 'sifting and sorting' fairly, schools reward middle-class values. The working class lack the cultural capital needed for success and so end up in working-class jobs.

Evaluation

- + Statistics and sociological research support the claim that meritocracy is a myth.
- + Demonstrates how individuals within the education system are influenced by structural factors, particularly the economy.
- + Illustrates how the role of education can be used to pass on ruling-class ideology that supports capitalism.
- − Internal criticism. Neo-Marxist **Willis** agrees that cultural reproduction occurs but argues that the working class are active and can see through the myth of meritocracy. The working-class 'lads' developed an anti-school culture which, although it led to their failure, showed how the hidden curriculum can be rejected by pupils.
- − Functionalists argue that the education system is not controlled by the capitalist economic system but offers equal opportunities for all. It is based on consensus not conflict.

Exam tip

For A-level in particular be prepared to link the topic of education to the general theoretical view that functionalists have of society. For example, Parsons argues that education is an important subsystem of the social structure that influences the individual.

Knowledge check 1

Outline three ways in which schools can prepare young people for the world of work.

Cultural capital The middle-class values, knowledge and experiences that are valued by the education system and are required for success in the examination system.

- Interactionists argue that (with the exception of Willis) Marxists ignore the role of individuals in education.
- Feminists argue that patriarchy within education is ignored. The hidden curriculum reinforces gender inequalities in subject choice, for example.
- Postmodernists argue that the Marxist view is out of date and that the correspondence principle does not exist. The role of education in a postmodern society is to ensure diversity not inequality.

Key concepts

ideological state apparatus; legitimation; cultural reproduction; correspondence principle; hidden curriculum; myth of meritocracy; cultural capital

New Right

Key ideas

- This is a political and sociological perspective that shares and develops some of the ideas of functionalism. See Table 1.

Similar to functionalist view	Different to the functionalist view
Agrees with the selection function. The more talented should be rewarded and allocated the most important jobs.	Education is not fulfilling the economic function. Too few school leavers have the skills needed for the global economy.
Agrees with the socialisation function. Education should pass on shared values to ensure a common culture.	Disagrees that the state can run the education system efficiently to meet the needs of pupils, parents and employers.
Agrees that the education system should be based on meritocracy and competition.	Greater competition is needed to improve standards in the education system.

Table 1 New Right ideas in relation to functionalism

- Thatcher's government introduced a range of **marketisation** policies in the 1988 **Education Reform Act** (ERA) which were designed to introduce market forces into the education system. Chubb and Moe (1990) argued that state-run education needed to be run more like a business with greater competition between schools that had to respond to the needs of their consumers (parents).
- David (1993) described marketised education as a **'parentocracy'**, meaning parents would have the right to choose schools for their children and were given information to do so via **Ofsted reports** and **league tables**.
- Schools were given greater powers to be independent by being able to control their own budgets and to **opt out** of local education authority (LEA) control. **Open enrolment** meant schools could recruit more pupils and receive greater funding as a result of **formula funding**.
- The New Right advocates greater diversity in the education system and would support the move towards the greater involvement of the private sector (**privatisation**) in the education system such as an increase in the number of academies and business sponsorship.
- In order to respond to the needs of the changing global economy there was also a greater emphasis on **vocational education** in order that young people were more prepared for the world of work (such as vocational AS and A-levels).

Key thinkers

Althusser, Bowles and Gintis, Bourdieu, Willis

Knowledge check 2

Outline two ways in which cultural capital can lead to middle-class pupils achieving higher levels than working-class pupils.

Formula funding Where schools receive funding based on the number of students they attract.

Evaluation

+ Policies influenced by the New Right have made education more responsive to the needs of the economy and created greater diversity in education and training.
+ Supporters argue that the continual improvement in exam results is evidence that increased competition as a result of marketisation policies between schools has improved standards.
- **Ball** argues that there is a 'myth of parentocracy' and that in reality middle-class parents benefit from marketisation policies. As **Gerwitz** suggests, working-class parents may lack the cultural and economic capital to be 'skilled choosers'.
- Marketisation has created an unequal, 'two-tier' state education system. Whereas popular schools are better funded and can attract more able, usually middle-class pupils, 'failing schools' cannot afford to be selective and may find it difficult to improve performance due to reduced funding and their inability to attract more able pupils.

Postmodernism

Key ideas

- The economy has moved from being **Fordist** (based on assembly-line mass production) to **post-Fordist** (which is increasingly **fragmented** and has to respond to the needs of the global market).
- The role of the education system has similarly had to shift from a 'one size fits all' provision (typified by comprehensive schools popular in the 1960s, see page 23) to the **diverse** range of education and training that reflects consumer choice and the needs of the ever-changing economy.
- Postmodernists point to the impact that globalisation had has on society, the economy and the education system. For example, many academy chains (see page 25) are controlled by companies from the USA, which has resulted in American-based behaviour management policies and teaching techniques being implemented. The increase in the number of overseas students has had an impact on the types of courses offered in higher education (e.g. more in medical sciences).
- Postmodernists argue that 'modern' theories such as functionalism and Marxism are out of date due to the impact of factors such as globalisation. They are particularly critical of Marxists as they see both the economy and the education system as being diverse rather than being based on class inequality.

Exam tip

Be prepared to link factors such as the increase in globalisation and privatisation and relate them to sociological theory. For example, New Right polices that have led to the increased influence of the private sector have brought about the diversity in the education system suggested by postmodernists, such as the growth of academies.

Key concepts

marketisation;
parentocracy;
consumer choice;
competition;
privatisation;
formula funding

Knowledge check 3

Outline three criticisms of the marketisation of education.

Globalisation
The increased interconnectedness in the world, characterised by international corporations and the global media.

Evaluation

+ Postmodernists are right to point out that society has become more diverse and that the economy requires workers to be more adaptable and have transferable skills.
+ Recent government and school policies have reflected increased diversity and flexibility in educational provision (e.g. specialist schools, academies, free schools, faith schools, lifelong learning, personalised timetables).
- Marxists argue that postmodernists ignore class inequality in the education system and wider society.
- Education is still largely under state control; is it really that diverse?

Key concepts

diversity;
fragmentation;
globalisation;
post-Fordism

Knowledge check 4

Outline two criticisms of the postmodern view that the education system is characterised by diversity.

Summary

After studying this section, you should be able to explain the role and purpose of education, including its relationship to the economy and to the class structure. You should be familiar with the main perspectives:

- Functionalism focuses on the positive contributions of the education system in maintaining social order in society and preparing and allocating individuals to their future role in the economy.
- Marxism focuses on how the education system oppresses pupils and reproduces and legitimates inequality between the social classes.

- The New Right emphasises how the marketisation of the education system is required in order that it meets the needs of pupils, parents and the economy.
- Postmodernists argue that the education system has developed to reflect the diverse needs of a post-Fordist economy.
- Feminists argue that all other theories ignore gender inequalities and that the education system reproduces patriarchal power in society.

■ Class differences in achievement

Social class has a significant impact on a child's educational achievement. Students from professional backgrounds are significantly more likely to achieve 5 A*–C grades at GCSE and enter higher education than those from unskilled backgrounds. As well as being more likely to stay on at school at 16, middle-class pupils are more likely to start school being able to read than pupils from disadvantaged backgrounds. Different reasons have been put forward for this social class gap in achievement.

External factors

Material deprivation

- This involves a lack of money to afford basic necessities.
- Working-class families are much more likely to be in poverty due to factors such as unemployment or a low income. They therefore may lack the money to afford resources which help academic success, such as internet access, paying for school trips or study books etc.

Exam tip

Be prepared to evaluate each of these factors by referring to various polices and interventions aimed at tackling material deprivation such as bursaries, student grants for higher education, schools subsidising school trips, school and public libraries loaning textbooks etc.

- They will be less able to afford private tuition and higher education costs.
- Poor diet can lead to absence through ill-health and low levels of concentration.
- Poor living conditions can lead to poor health and absence from school. It can also mean a lack of space to study due to overcrowding.
- Government statistics show that those receiving free school meals consistently underachieve demonstrating the correlation between material deprivation and academic success.

Cultural deprivation

- Cultural deprivation refers to a lack of the 'correct' values, attitudes and skills needed for academic success. It is claimed that working-class parents often fail to socialise their children into these values.
- Sociologists such as functionalists and the New Right would argue that the working-class culture (and underclass culture for the New Right) and parenting are not aimed at educational success.
- Compared to their middle-class counterparts, working-class parents are less likely to encourage **intellectual development** by reading to their children or engaging in educational activities.
- **Douglas** (1964) argued that working-class parents had lower aspirations. He claimed that this was demonstrated by the fact that they were less likely than middle-class parents to go to parents' evenings.
- **Sugarman** (1970) argues that working-class culture is characterised by values such as **immediate gratification** (wanting rewards now) and fatalism that act as a barrier to achievement. For example, working-class parents would encourage their children to leave school as soon as possible in order to earn money rather than study hard.
- Conversely, middle-class parents would encourage their children to **defer gratification** (postpone rewards) by staying in education as long as possible to gain qualifications.
- **Bernstein** (1970) argued that the working class underachieve as they tend to use only the **restricted code** which is based on short forms of speech, whereas the middle class are also socialised into the **elaborated code** which is the language used by teachers and the school curriculum. Therefore middle-class students are more likely to achieve, particularly in subjects such as English.

Theories of cultural and material deprivation have had an influence on government policy in the form of **compensatory education** in the 1960s. Operation Head Start in the USA was influenced by cultural deprivation theory and was aimed at changing the values of low income parents in order to better prepare pre-school children for school. In the UK compensatory education began with **Educational Priority Areas** where the government allocated additional resources to four low-income inner-city areas. More recently New Labour attempted to tackle social exclusion with policies such as **Education Action Zones** and **Sure Start** (see page 24).

Exam tip

Particularly for A-level, you should make the link between sociological theory and government educational policies. Compensatory policies such as Operation Head Start were based on the functionalist belief that educational underachievement was caused by poor socialisation at home.

Knowledge check 5

Outline three material factors that may negatively affect the educational achievement of working-class students.

Fatalism The idea that there is nothing you can do to change your situation (such as working hard in school).

Social exclusion Social exclusion is where individuals or groups of people are blocked from rights, opportunities and resources that are normal to other members of society. Policies to combat social exclusion aim to re-integrate excluded people back into society.

Cultural capital

■ Marxist **Bourdieu** (1971, 1984) argued that middle-class pupils achieve more as they possess the language, values and skills that are rewarded by the education system. This he called **cultural capital**. For example, a knowledge of Shakespeare and the 'arts', that upper- and middle-class parents may have socialised their children into, will be rewarded and seen as valuable by schools.

■ Bourdieu argues that as well as having more economic capital, i.e. financial resources, the middle class are more likely to possess the cultural capital needed to succeed in education. He also argued that this was passed on from one generation to the next, resulting in **cultural reproduction**.

Evaluation

Cultural deprivation	Material deprivation
Douglas is right to suggest that middle-class parents may have higher aspirations for their children due to their own higher levels of education. If a child's parent does not attend a parents' evening, this may send the message that the child does not need to try hard at school.	Is attending parents' evenings a good measure of parental interest? Working-class parents may not attend due to having to work shifts or may not be able to afford the costs of attending such as transport or babysitting. They may also be put off by what they feel is the middle-class atmosphere of the school.
Sugarman is right to argue that middle-class parents are likely to socialise their children to defer gratification and will place a higher value on education as they themselves are more likely to have gone to university.	The working class are being realistic not fatalistic. Rather than not valuing education, they may have no choice but to ask their children to leave school as they need them to earn money for the family.
A poor diet is based more on cultural choices than a lack of money. A healthy diet does not have to be expensive.	Working-class families may not be able to afford the healthy diet that is essential to help children achieve.
Cultural deprivation theorists are correct to argue that the working class not buying educational toys may have a negative impact on developing intellectual skills and hence achievement.	Working-class parents may not buy educational toys because they are more expensive not because they are not interested in developing their children intellectually.

Table 2 A comparison of cultural and material explanations

+ A strength of **Bernstein** is that, unlike other cultural deprivation theorists, he acknowledges that the school has a role in working-class underachievement. He argues that the school is to blame for not teaching them the elaborate code. However, the significance of possessing the elaborate code may not be as important in all subjects, such as maths.

- **Keddie** (1973) criticises cultural deprivation for adopting a 'victim-blaming' approach. She argues that working-class culture is different not inferior. The same criticism can be applied to working-class language codes.

+ A strength of **Bourdieu** is that he emphasised the importance of both cultural and economic factors. However, material deprivation theorists argue that he overestimates the importance of cultural factors. For example, rather than a lack of cultural capital, a lack of money is more likely to prevent a working-class student going to university due to the high cost of tuition fees. Also, is culture automatically passed on, as Bourdieu suggests?

- Not all working-class students fail and external explanations ignore the impact of school-based factors.

Knowledge check 6

What is the difference between cultural capital and cultural deprivation?

Internal factors

Interactionists look at a range of processes within school that can affect differential class achievement.

Labelling

Becker (1971) argued that teachers (who are mainly middle class) evaluated pupils in terms of an **'ideal pupil'**, reflecting middle-class attitudes, values and speech codes. Working-class pupils were more likely to be negatively labelled by teachers and seen as 'deviant pupils'.

Self-fulfilling prophecy

Rosenthal and Jacobsen (1968) argued that negative labelling can lead to a self-fulfilling prophecy of failure. If students are negatively labelled by a teacher they may develop a negative self-image, see themselves as a failure, and so give up and underachieve.

Streaming

Due to labelling, working-class pupils are more likely to be put in a lower **stream** and so underachieve. **Keddie** (1971) felt that by being placed in lower streams working-class pupils were being denied the knowledge they needed for success.

Gillborn and Youdell (2001) argued that the pressure on schools to improve their league table position (the **A-to-C economy**) led to the adoption a different form of streaming. Educational triage occurred where no help was given to students viewed as 'hopeless cases', whereas additional resources such as mentoring support was given to pupils on the C/D border. As a result of labelling, working-class (and black) students were more likely to be placed in bottom sets and sit lower-tier GCSEs, even though they had similar grades to middle-class and white students.

Subculture

- **Lacey** (1970) argued that as a response to labelling, polarisation occurs whereby those positively labelled by teachers, mainly middle-class pupils, would adopt a **pro-school** subculture, whereas those negatively labelled, mainly working-class pupils, would adopt an **anti-school** subculture which would lead to failure.
- **Woods** (1984) adopted a more sophisticated approach and argued that there were eight types of **pupils' adaptations** to labelling and streaming. For example, 'compliance' was mainly a pro-education response but pupils would only comply with teachers for their own reasons such as exam success.

Marxist views of processes within school:
- A study by **Willis** showed how the anti-school culture of the working-class 'lads' meant that they would fail and end up in working-class jobs. This subculture did not result from teacher labelling, however, but from the 'lads' manual working-class values.
- **Bowles and Gintis** argued that the correspondence principle and the hidden curriculum, with their emphasis on competition and accepting authority, were processes in school that favoured middle-class students and prepared them for their future roles such as managerial positions (see page 8).

Exam tip

These factors can also be applied to differential achievement based on ethnicity and gender.

Self-fulfilling prophecy When people act out a label: they behave in the way they know others have predicted.

Streaming When schools group students together by ability for all subjects.

Exam tip

Refer to how the issue of pupil identities can also affect the experience of different ethnic groups in school (see p. 22).

Polarisation Where two opposite extremes are created. For example, teacher labelling may lead to students joining two types of subculture, pro- or anti-school.

Particularly for the A-level exam, be prepared to make links between sociological theory and methods (see page 27). Willis is described as a neo-Marxist as he combines Marxist theory with interpretivist methods favoured by interactionists. By using group interviews and observation, Willis felt he was able to uncover the meanings behind why the 'lads' resisted the values of the school.

Policies

In addition to the above internal factors, **educational policies** also influence processes in schools and affect differential class achievement. Sociologists such as Marxists would argue that marketisation policies, with their emphasis on greater selection, have increased the class gap in achievement (see page 23). **Bartlett** (1993) argues that these policies enable schools high up in the league tables to **'cream-skim'** higher ability students who are more likely to be middle class. They can also **'silt-shift'** less able students to schools lower in the league tables. These less able students are likely to be working-class pupils who will then have less opportunity to be successful in a lower-achieving school.

Evaluation of internal explanations

+ Interactionists demonstrate the importance of how labelling and other processes in schools can lead to inequalities in achievement between the social classes. They highlight a range of different strategies that students can adopt, which enable them to achieve status through alternative means.
− Internal criticism. Labelling and the self-fulfilling prophecy are too deterministic. As **Fuller's** study shows, students can reject negative teacher labels and achieve (see page 18). Rather than a self-fulfilling prophecy of failure, students can adopt a self-negating prophecy of success.
− Cultural deprivation theorists argue that subcultures develop from the poor values of the working class rather than processes in schools.
− Marxists argue that interactionists fail to take account of external factors, namely how differential class achievement is caused by inequalities in capitalist society.
− Interactionist research is not representative as it is usually based on the experiences of one school so cannot be generalised.

Exam tip

Be prepared to evaluate evidence by relating its relevance to contemporary issues in education. While streaming is less common than in the 1970s, when interactionist research was prominent, working-class pupils today may still be more likely to be placed in lower sets and therefore entered for lower-tier exams.

Deterministic The view that human behaviour is directed and determined by forces beyond the control of the individual.

Knowledge check 7

Outline two criticisms of the view that teacher labelling results in pupils joining anti-school subcultures.

Summary

After studying this section, you should be able to explain differential educational achievement of social groups by social class in contemporary society and the relationships and processes within schools in relation to social class. You should be familiar with the following suggested explanations:
  ■ external factors including material deprivation, cultural deprivation, language speech codes, cultural capital

  ■ internal factors including processes in schools such as teacher/pupil relationships, labelling, pupil identities and subcultures, and the organisation of teaching and learning, setting and streaming, the curriculum (both official and hidden) and educational polices

■ Ethnic differences in achievement

In terms of ethnic groups the highest achievers are students from Chinese, African Asian (Indian in origin) and Indian backgrounds, whereas those from black, Pakistani and Bangladeshi backgrounds do worst. However, differential ethnic achievement is a very complex issue and is also influenced by social class and gender. For example, both black and white working-class boys are low achievers while Bangladeshi and Pakistani women are the least well qualified.

External factors

Material deprivation

Material deprivation theorists argue that there is a link between a lack of financial resources and achievement.

- As Pakistani and Bangladeshi pupils are from the poorest ethnic minority groups they are more likely to be affected by a lack of material resources.
- The **Swann Report** (1985) felt that socio-economic factors affected the lower levels of achievement of Afro-Caribbean pupils.
- Discrimination often experienced by ethnic minority groups in the wider society, in employment and housing in particular, may contribute to levels of material deprivation experienced.
- As Chinese, African Asian and Indian pupils are less likely to be on a low income or unemployed, they are less likely to experience material deprivation.

Cultural deprivation

Cultural deprivation theorists argue that there is a link between a lack of the 'correct' values and educational successes.

- Cultural deprivation theorists argue that white working-class pupils are among the lowest-achieving groups due to a lack of parental support and negative attitudes towards education (see page 12).
- Cultural deprivation theorists argue that children from black and other ethnic minority backgrounds often have a lack of Standard English and so are at a disadvantage in school. Bereiter and Engelmann (1966) felt that the language of low-income black Americans was a barrier to achievement in school.
- **Murray** (1984) argued that many black boys underachieve due to not having a male role model at home as approximately half of black-Caribbean families are single parent.
- **Pryce** (1979) described the structure of black-Caribbean families being 'turbulent' and argued that unlike Asian culture, black-Caribbean culture was less resistant to racism, which means that black pupils may lack self-esteem and so underachieve.

Evaluation of external factors

+ The **Swann Report** found that at least half of the difference in achievement between ethnic groups was due to social class, supporting the importance of material deprivation.
+ Language barriers are going to affect the achievement of pupils whose first language is not English, particularly those who have recently migrated to the UK.
- Material deprivation does not explain all differences between ethnic minority groups. For example, white and Asian middle-class pupils do better than black middle-class pupils.
- Research suggests that language is not a key factor. **Driver and Ballard** (1981) found that Asian pupils whose first language was not English had caught up by the age of 16. Also schools offer additional support for students whose first language is not English (referred to as EAL support — English as an additional language).
- **Connor** (2004) found that parents from all ethnic minority groups placed a higher value on the importance of their children attending higher education than white parents.
- Female-headed households, with independent, career-minded Afro-Caribbean women, may act as a positive role model for black girls, helping them to achieve.
- **Khan** (1979) argues that Asian families are 'controlling', particularly for girls, and that this may act as a barrier to success rather being a positive resource.
- Not all parents from ethnic minority backgrounds suffer from cultural deprivation. 'Tiger mums', with their emphasis on the importance of education, may help to explain the high achievement of Chinese pupils. **Driver and Ballard** (1981) felt that Asian families were a 'positive resource' due to high levels of parental expectations which increased achievement levels.
- **Mirza** (1992) found that it was not a lack of self-esteem that caused the black girls to underachieve. The group she studied had a pro-education subculture, but they failed as they were unwilling to ask for help from teachers, who they saw as racist.
- **Keddie** is critical of cultural deprivation theory (see page 13) and argues that ethnic minorities cannot be deprived of their own culture. She argues that internal factors, such as schools being ethnocentric, are the cause of ethnic minorities underachieving.

Internal factors

Labelling

■ **Gillborn and Youdell** (2000) found that teachers had 'racialised expectations' which resulted in black students being negatively labelled as a 'threat'. They felt that black boys were more likely to be excluded or put in bottom sets as a result.
■ **Wright** (1992) found that Asian pupils were excluded and received less attention from teachers having been labelled as having poor language skills. They failed as a result of the negative impact this had on their self-esteem.

Exam tip

Be prepared to link external to internal factors. While disagreeing with cultural deprivation theorists, interactionists argue that teachers may negatively label students who have English as a second language or who have a different accent as having less ability and therefore place them in lower sets.

Exam tip

As with social class you should be prepared to analyse how concepts such as labelling, self-fulfilling prophecy, subcultures and streaming interact and relate to ethnicity and achievement. If ethnic minority students are negatively labelled they may be more likely to be placed in a lower set or stream, join an anti-school subculture and underachieve as a result.

Subcultures

- **Sewell** (1988) found that there were four types of pupil responses that black boys would adapt to as a result of being negatively labelled by teachers as anti-school. The 'rebels' lived up to this label, formed an anti-school subculture and failed. However this response was rare and the largest group was the 'conformists' who adopted pro-school attitudes and worked hard to achieve.
- Like Sewell's 'innovators', **Fuller's** (1984) black girls adopted a pro-education, anti-school subculture and worked hard to achieve but rejected teacher labels and didn't seek their approval.

The ethnocentric curriculum

- Some sociologists have argued that the curriculum in British schools reflects white, middle-class culture over others. Subjects such as history and religious education are seen as being taught from a British, Christian perspective and have marginalised the history of ethnic minorities.
- **Coard** (1971) argues that the ethnocentric curriculum is an example of institutional racism in British schools which makes black students feel inferior and lowers their self-esteem and achievement as a result.

Educational policies

Marketisation policies allowing increased selection can viewed as another form of institutional racism as they may discriminate against certain ethnic minority groups. For example black-Caribbean pupils, particularly boys, may be seen as 'less attractive' to higher-achieving schools due to their perceived negative impact on their league table position. As a result their achievement may be negatively affected due to them going to less popular, 'failing' schools.

Institutional racism
Where policies and attitudes of an institution, such as a school or college, unintentionally discriminate against ethnic minority groups.

Exam tip

When looking at ethnicity and achievement you should be prepared to discuss the interplay between ethnicity, class and gender. While class may be less significant for the lower achievement of black boys, it may have an impact on the achievement of Indian girls.

Evaluation of internal factors

- As with social class (see page 15) a problem with teacher labelling as an explanation for ethnic differences in underachievement is that it is deterministic as the self-fulfilling prophecy may not occur. As **Mirza, Fuller** and **Sewell's** studies illustrate, students may respond to teacher labels in a variety of different ways.
- Cultural deprivation theorists would argue that higher exclusion rates for black boys are caused by their poor behaviour, stemming from inadequate socialisation, rather than teacher labelling.
- Other external factors may also be an important cause of underachievement. **Sewell** acknowledges that as well as teacher labelling, black boys' achievement may be influenced by an absence of positive role models.

- For example as well as a lack of a male role model at home, black boys may be influenced by the macho, 'gangsta' image of black males, promoted by the media, which does not place value on educational success.
- Internal explanations also ignore the impact that racism in wider society may have on achievement.
- Critics of the claim that the curriculum in British schools is ethnocentric would point to the introduction of multicultural education policies into schools and subjects such as religious education that teaches world religions as part of the National Curriculum. Also Chinese students are the highest-achieving ethnic group despite their culture being largely ignored in the curriculum.

Exam tip

You can develop evaluation by referring to different theoretical criticisms of factors that affect achievement. In terms of selection policies Marxist influenced sociologists would argue that rather than being culturally deprived such as having language barriers, ethnic minorities may lack the cultural capital required to get their child into the higher-achieving schools.

Knowledge check 9

Outline two examples of institutional racism that may affect the achievement of ethnic minority groups.

Summary

After studying this section, you should be able to explain differential educational achievement of social groups by ethnicity in contemporary society and the relationships and processes within schools relating to ethnicity. You should be familiar with the following:
- external factors including material deprivation, cultural deprivation, language speech codes, cultural capital and racism in wider society
- internal factors including processes in schools such as teacher/pupil relationships, labelling, pupil identities and subcultures, the organisation of teaching and learning, setting and streaming, the ethnocentric curriculum and educational polices

■ Gender differences in achievement and subject choice

While boys used to achieve higher than girls, since the 1980s they have fallen behind. Girls are now achieving better results than boys at every level and in most subjects. Despite this, there are still some gender differences in subject choice, particularly at post-16. While boys tend to choose subjects such as science and technology, for example, girls tend to opt for arts and humanities based subjects. Tables 3a and 3b contain possible ways in which the factor in the left-hand column could be developed with AO2 or AO3 points. (See pages 51–52 for more specific information on assessment objectives.)

Exam tip

For questions on boys' underachievement, you should refer to the fact that while the gender gap has increased over the past 30 years, boys' achievement has also increased considerably over this period.

The 'gender gap' in achievement

External factors	Assessment objectives (AOs)
The influence of feminism This has raised awareness about gender inequality in society. 'Girl power' has made girls more independent.	AO2 This has caused a change in female expectations which has made girls value education more. AO3 Radical feminists argue that patriarchy still exists.
Changing priorities Sharpe (1994) found that between 1974 and 1994 girls' priorities switched from love and marriage to careers and supporting themselves.	AO2 This change in aspirations and wanting to be financially independent requires girls to work hard in school in order to gain qualifications.
Changes in the family The number of female lone-parent families has increased.	AO2 'Working mums' act as role models and do inspire girls to achieve.
Changes in women's employment Legislation such as the Equal Pay and Sex Discrimination Acts have created more equality and increased the proportion of women in employment.	AO2 Increased opportunities in employment have given the incentive for girls to work hard in school. AO3 The pay gap between the sexes still exists. There is still a glass ceiling in many employment sectors.

Table 3a External factors that help to explain the 'gender gap' in achievement

Internal factors	Assessment objectives (AOs)
Educational policies Governments have introduced a range of policies that have led to equal opportunities for girls in education.	AO2/3 GIST and the National Curriculum (see page 23) have improved girls' participation and achievement in subjects such as science. Barriers have been removed.
Positive role models in schools The number of female teachers and head teachers has increased.	AO3 While the majority of heads at primary are female, most secondary heads are male.
Changes in assessment AS and A-levels and GCSEs introduced more coursework and modular exams which favoured girls.	AO2 Coursework did raise girls' achievement due to girls being more organised than boys. AO3 Less coursework and a return to final exams.
Teacher labelling Research suggests that teachers have lower expectations of boys and give more positive attention to girls.	AO2 This may lead to a self-fulfilling prophecy of failure for boys but raise the achievement of girls. AO3 This research is dated and may not apply today.
Fewer stereotypes in the curriculum Gender stereotypes were removed from resources.	AO2 Fewer sexist images of females in textbooks may raise aspirations and therefore achievement of girls.
Selection policies Marketisation policies (see page 23) have meant that boys are less attractive to higher-achieving schools.	AO2 Girls are more likely to get into a 'good' school and so have a greater opportunity to achieve than boys.

Table 3b Internal factors that help to explain the 'gender gap' in achievement

GIST Girls into Science and Technology — a government policy aimed at encouraging girls to pursue a career in traditional male areas.

Glass ceiling The invisible barrier that women have to 'break through' in order to obtain high positions in the labour market.

Exam tip

To develop analysis you should refer to how the same factors may impact differently on the achievement of girls and boys. While female single parents may act as a positive role model for girls, they might mean a lack of a positive male role model at home for boys. Similarly, the internal factors that have helped raise females' achievement may have had a negative impact on boys.

Exam tip

In an essay question on achievement in relation to either gender, class or ethnicity, be prepared to state which factor you feel is the most important influence. This would be a useful strategy to employ in a conclusion.

External factors	Assessment objectives (AOs)
Boys' lack of literacy skills While girls have a 'bedroom culture' which promotes literacy and communication skills, boys read less and tend to engage in more active leisure activities.	AO2 If reading is seen by boys as 'girly' it will have a negative impact in subjects, especially English. AO3 There have been policies introduced to encourage boys to read, e.g. 'Reading Champions'.
Fewer 'male' jobs As a result of globalisation there has been a decline in the number of traditional 'male' jobs in manufacturing. Boys are having an 'identity crisis' as they may no longer be future breadwinners.	AO2 The rise in male unemployment may lead to boys not seeing the point of education and failing. AO3 Will boys make the connection between working hard in school and the types of jobs they wish to do when they leave school?
Lack of male role models at home	AO3 Does this mean that boys value education less?
Internal factors	**Assessment objectives (AOs)**
Feminisation of education Coursework and a lack of male teachers, particularly at primary level.	AO3 Francis (2006) found that the gender of teachers was not important to most primary school students.
Laddish subcultures Mac an Ghaill (1994) argues that boys are more likely than girls to join anti-school subcultures. As with Willis' 'lads', these subcultures may be caused by external factors.	AO2 If boys are more concerned about being negatively labelled by peers (e.g. as 'gay') if they try hard in school, this will reduce achievement. AO3 This may only apply to working-class boys.

Table 4 Factors that relate to the underachievement of boys

Subject choice

External	AO2: Application to subject choice
Early gender socialisation Norman (1988) notes how sex stereotyping occurs in terms of the types of toys bought and the types of play that boys and girls are encouraged to engage in.	If boys are given construction based toys they are more likely to opt for resistant materials. Conversely, if girls are given dolls and kitchen sets they are more likely to pick health and social care.
Gendered career opportunities Sex stereotyping occurs in jobs, such as IT being seen as a male domain and the 'caring' professions being for females.	As a result, boys and girls are more likely to opt for subjects that relate to these careers, e.g. childcare and food technology for girls and computing for boys.
Internal	**AO2: Application to subject choice**
Gendered subject images Kelly (1987) felt that science was presented as a masculine subject by teachers. Research suggests that subjects such as science are taught in ways that favour boys.	As a result, girls are less likely to opt for science subjects. However, in single sex schools, more girls opt for traditional 'male' subjects, which suggests the school may have an influence on subject images.
Peer pressure As well as teachers and parents, pupils are likely to be influenced by their peers to choose gender stereotypical subjects.	Boys may be less likely to opt for subjects such as dance if they are called 'gay' by their friends. However, such stereotypes are increasingly less common today.

Table 5 Factors affecting gender and subject choice

Exam tip

You can also develop analysis by explaining how factors that influence subject choice may link together. For example, as the image of subjects such as dance become less stereotypically female, it is less likely that boys will receive negative comments from their peers if they opt for them.

Exam tip

Particularly for A-level, be prepared to link factors to different feminist theoretical perspectives. For example, while liberal feminists would argue that policies such as the Equal Pay Act and GIST have been largely successful in bringing about greater equality for females, radical feminists would argue that the education system is still based on patriarchy as it continues to limit females' subject and career choices.

Exam tip

The division into external and internal is helpful but may be artificial. Develop analysis by discussing how the two may overlap.

Knowledge check 10

Outline three ways in which gender socialisation may influence subject choice.

Summary

After studying this section, you should be able to explain differential educational achievement and subject choice of social groups by gender in contemporary society and the relationships and processes within schools relating to gender. You should be familiar with the following:

- external factors including changes in the family, women's employment and girls' priorities; gender socialisation at home and in society and the impact of feminism

- internal factors including processes in schools such as teacher/pupil relationships, labelling, pupil identities and subcultures, the organisation of teaching and learning, the feminisation of education, gender socialisation in school and educational polices

Identity: class, ethnicity and gender

- Identity refers to how individuals see themselves and how they are seen by others. It is complex and is shaped not only by factors such as gender, class and ethnicity but also issues such as sexuality and different types of consumption and leisure patterns. As Willis' study on the 'lads' demonstrates, working-class identities can have a negative impact on achievement. **Hollingsworth and Williams** (2009) found that male working-class subcultures are now seen by other pupils (not themselves) as 'chavs' rather than 'lads' and that mainly middle-class subcultures such as 'emos', 'goths' and 'skaters' are influenced by different types of music.

- **Archer et al.** (2010) argued that the identity of working-class pupils is based on ways of thinking that can be very different from the middle-class habitus of the school. While dress styles such as 'low-riding' trousers, baseball caps and sports designer wear such as Nike may generate self-worth for the working-class pupil, this would come into conflict with the dress codes of the school.

- They argued that many working-class pupils see education as being alien to them and that in order to be successful they would have to 'give up' their working-class identity, which they recognise that the school devalues. As a result, some may choose **self-exclusion** from typical middle-class lifestyle choices such as higher education but instead actively 'resist through rituals' by heavily investing in their **'Nike' identity**. This conflict with the school's habitus has a negative impact on the achievement of working-class students who chose not to conform to the middle-class habitus of the education system.

- From interviews and focus groups with teachers, pupils and parents in secondary schools, **Archer** (2008) found that ethnic-minority groups were excluded from the ideal pupil identity, which was seen as white, middle-class, male and 'normal' in terms of sexuality. Despite being successful, Chinese pupils were viewed as being too passive, quiet and repressed (females) or effeminate (males) and therefore the 'wrong' sort of learner.

- Archer identified two other pupil identities: the 'pathologised' (abnormal), which was the hard-working, conformist Asian pupil with an oppressed sexuality; and the 'demonised', which was the culturally and intellectually inferior black or white working-class pupil with an inappropriate, 'excessive' sexuality. Archer's study illustrated the complex nature of the beliefs held by teachers regarding pupil identities, which involved an interplay between ethnicity, class, gender and sexuality.

- **Radical feminists** argue that schools reinforce gender and sexual identities, which helps to promote a hegemonic masculinity. **Lees** (1986 and 1993) identified how this occurs through **double standards** and **verbal abuse**. Whereas girls are negatively labelled as 'slags', 'sluts' and 'slappers', boys would be viewed as 'studs' for the same sexual behaviour. Lees argued that these double standards and name-calling help to shape and justify male power. Research suggests that verbal abuse of girls was often ignored and unchallenged by teachers, therefore reinforcing hegemonic definitions of gender identity.

- Verbal abuse may also be used to reinforce masculine identities by male peer groups. **Mac an Ghaill** (1994) found that working-class 'macho lads' referred to working-class boys who worked hard as 'dickhead achievers'. **Epstein** (1998) and Willis showed how working-class boys who want to achieve may be the victims of verbal abuse and be labelled as effeminate or 'gay'.

Habitus A term developed by Bourdieu to describe socialised norms or tendencies that guide behaviour and thinking that are shared by a particular social class.

Hegemonic masculinity How males maintain dominant social roles over women and other gender identities.

■ Educational policies

- The 1944 Education Act introduced secondary education for all, based on the notion that there should be three types of school that would reflect the needs of three types of intelligence. The tripartite system as it was known was **based on selection** as entry to the different types of school (grammar, technical or modern) depended on performance in the 11+ exam. It was based on the notion that intelligence was fixed at birth, and that the 11+ exam could correctly place children into one of three main intelligence groups.
- While this policy was aimed at **reducing class inequalities**, selection based on the 11+ exam was thought to favour middle-class students. From 1965, the tripartite system was largely replaced by the **comprehensive system**, which was **non-selective** as there was no entry exam. This policy was again aimed at reducing **class inequalities** as all children were meant to get equal opportunities and attend their local school.

1988 Education Reform Act (ERA)

- The 1988 ERA introduced a range of policies that were influenced by the New Right's view that **marketisation** and **privatisation** of the education system were required to improve standards, increase competition and choice and make schools more responsive to the needs of the global economy. Policies of parental choice, opting out, formula funding and open enrolment meant a **return to selection** (see page 9).
- A **National Curriculum** of compulsory subjects for all 5- to 16-year-olds was introduced.
- Pupils had to sit national tests (SATs), initially at 7, 11 and 14.
- **League tables** for SATs and GCSEs and **Ofsted reports** were to be published, which parents could use to make an informed choice on where to send their children.
- **City Technology Colleges** (CTCs) were forerunners of academies. They reflected the New Right's drive towards the privatisation of education as they were outside of local authority control, part funded by private businesses and had great powers of selection.

New Labour policies (1997–2010)

- New Labour's policies have been described as **'third way'** politics as they involve a mix of more traditional Labour policies, aimed at **reducing inequality** in achievement, but also incorporated the New Right's emphasis on **diversity and choice** and responding to the needs of the global economy.

- A key policy that continued the New Right's move towards greater **privatisation** in education was the 2000 Learning Skills Act, which introduced **academies**. These City Academies (later called Sponsored Academies) originally required private sponsorship with the aim of bringing 'private sector best practice and innovative management' into failing schools.

Policies influenced by the New Right	Policies aimed at reducing inequality
Establishing specialist schools that would give greater choice to parents	Sure Start programmes (including nursery schools) aimed at tackling social exclusion
Encouraging faith schools which were usually set up by single-faith groups	Education Action Zones — meant additional funding in areas of high social deprivation
Sponsored Academies — aimed at raising achievement through greater competition as well as providing greater choice	Education Maintenance Allowance (EMA) — this encouraged children from low income families to stay on in education at 16
Introducing tuition fees for higher education — meant that universities would face greater competition in order to attract students	AIM Higher — to encourage children from low income families to aspire to go on to higher education

Table 6 Key New Labour policies

- Another policy that was proposed was the raising of the participation age to 18. Pupils who left school at 16 would have to continue with some form of education or training. This policy was aimed at addressing inequality as it was an attempt to deal with the increasing number of 'Neets' (those '**n**ot in **e**ducation, **e**mployment or **t**raining') who were mainly from working-class backgrounds.
- In addition to these policies aimed at reducing inequality and increasing diversity and choice, New Labour continued the New Right's emphasis on promoting vocational education and training, particularly for disaffected students.

Exam tip

As well as trying to standardise assessments, the National Curriculum has had the knock-on effect of improving the achievement of girls in subjects like science which they could no longer opt out of. Having studied them for GCSE, it also meant that girls were more likely to opt for science subjects post-16, therefore also impacting on subject choice.

Conservative/Liberal Democrat coalition government 2010–15

- Under the 2010 Academies Act, the government invited all secondary schools to become '**Converter Academies**', which meant that schools would opt out of local authority control and receive all of their funding direct from government, with the option of buying services at a cheaper rate.
- The Act also introduced new academies, **Free Schools**, set up by 'founding groups' which included parents, education charities, businesses and religious groups.

- In 2012 the academy scheme was extended to primary schools.
- New Labour policies on reducing inequality were either scrapped, as in the case of EMA, or greatly reduced, as in the case of Sure Start provision. Also tuition fees (in England and Wales) were increased from £3,000 to a maximum of £9,000 per year.
- The **raising of the participation age** was introduced in two stages. Pupils who left Year 11 in the summer of 2014 or later had to continue with some form of education or training at least until their eighteenth birthday. If the education or training was part time, it had to be combined with at least 20 hours of employment or voluntary work.
- However, policies to reduce inequality were also introduced. The Pupil Premium in 2011 gave schools additional funding for each pupil from a disadvantaged background. In 2014–15 the Pupil Premium Plus meant schools received £1,900 for children who are looked after (in local authority care).

Globalisation, privatisation and education policies

- An inevitable consequence of the growth of **marketisation** polices has been an increase in the **privatisation** of the education system. By 2015, over two thirds of secondary schools had converted to academies and had therefore opted out of local authority control.
- Another example of the reduced role of local authorities has been the increased level of privatisation of educational services such as specialist behaviour and learning support.
- The New Labour policy of encouraging public–private partnerships (PPPs) facilitated the increasing involvement of private companies in the financing and building of state schools.
- Postmodernists (see page 10) would argue that recent policies promoting diversity and choice have allowed schools to be more flexible and better able to adapt to the changes faced in a postmodern society. For example, **globalisation** has led to an increase in migrant workers in the UK and schools have been able to respond to this by buying in additional EAL support for the increasing number of students whose first language is not English.
- Postmodernists would argue that schools and other educational institutions are now responding to the demands of a **post-Fordist** economy that has developed as a result of globalisation. For example, schools are offering personalised timetables and there has been an increase in more flexible approaches to education such as distance learning via the internet and lifelong learning.
- The global nature of privatisation in the education system is illustrated by the growth of international education management organisations such as EdisonLearning Inc. in the UK. This company based in the USA claims to be able to improve student achievement while making a profit for its shareholders.

Exam tip

You should be able to relate sociological theory to the impact that these policies may have on inequality in achievement. For example, a school with falling rolls and less funding will be less likely to afford to buy in services such as specialist learning and behaviour support. Marxists would argue that these are the very schools that need such support due to them being in deprived areas and less able to select high-achieving students.

Knowledge check 11

Outline two ways in which education has become more privatised.

Evaluation

+ Schools have become more accountable to parents as a result of New Right influenced marketisation policies. The publication of Ofsted reports and league tables has increased information for parents regarding the performance of schools.
+ There is some evidence to suggest that some academies have improved the performance of the struggling inner-city schools that they replaced.
+ Postmodernists would support New Labour's promotion of lifelong learning as it enabled adults to retrain to gain the skills required for the ever-changing needs of the economy.
+ New Labour did invest more money into education and had a range of policies aimed at reducing inequality, such as EAZs.
− Marxists would argue that New Labour policies may have had little impact on tackling structural inequalities in society in relation to both class and ethnic differences.
− It has been argued that there is a contradiction in New Labour policies. Whereas EMA and AIM Higher encouraged students from lower-income families to go into higher education, tuition fees, which such students may not have been able to afford, were introduced.
− As with compensatory policies such as Operation Head Start in the USA, New Labour's Sure Start programme has been accused of being patronising to the working class as it implies that their values are inferior and that they need help to be a 'good parent'.
− New Right policies of marketisation and parentocracy, continued to some extent by New Labour, have been accused of favouring the middle class (see page 9).

Summary

After studying this section, you should be able to explain the significance of educational policies. You should be familiar with the following:
- policies of selection, marketisation and privatisation
- polices aimed at achieving greater equality of opportunity of outcome and access to education
- the impact of sociological theory and globalisation on educational policy

■ Sociological research methods (AS and A-level)

Types of methods and data

Sociologists can use either **primary methods**, information collected by the researchers themselves, or **secondary methods**, information gathered by someone else. With primary methods, sociologists can gather the precise data they need, whereas existing data from secondary sources may not provide exactly what the sociologist requires. Data can also be divided into **quantitative**, which is in numerical form, or **qualitative**, which gives a detailed picture of people's opinions and meanings.

Exam tip

You should be able to compare the different types of data and methods. For example, while there is a lack of control with data from secondary methods, primary methods are more expensive and time-consuming.

Factors that influence choice of method

Theoretical issues

There are three key concepts that relate to theoretical issues:

- **Validity** refers to whether a method measures what it sets out to measure. Valid data is in-depth and will give a 'true picture' of reality.
- **Reliability** refers to whether a method can be repeated or **replicated**. Research is reliable if other sociologists using the same methods get the same results.
- **Representativeness** refers to whether the group studied is a true cross section of the population. If the sample used is **representative** sociologists can **generalise** the findings to the wider population.

Exam tip

Never state simplistically that a method is 'reliable and valid', particularly in a small-mark question. This will need qualifying and explaining as methods are usually one or the other.

As can be seen in Figure 1, there is a close relationship between these three concepts, the types of data and methods sociologists use and sociologists' **methodological and theoretical perspectives**.

Exam tip

A detailed knowledge of theory is not required for AS. For A-level you may be required to answer a 10-mark question on sociological theory in Paper 1.

Methodological perspective The sociologist's view of how the world should be studied. The two contrasting views are positivism and interpretivism.

Theoretical perspective The sociologist's view of the world. The main theories are Marxism, functionalism, interactionism and feminism. See section on sociological theory for more detail (page 41).

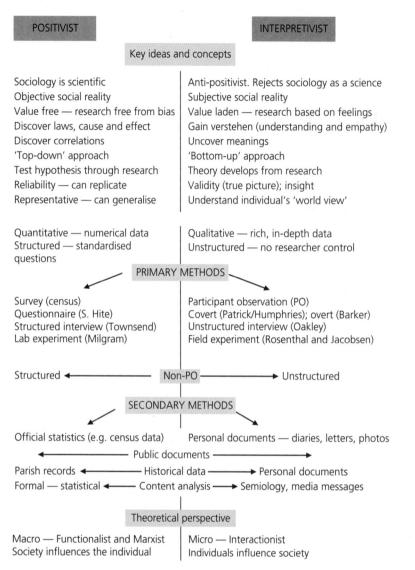

POSITIVIST   INTERPRETIVIST

Key ideas and concepts

POSITIVIST	INTERPRETIVIST
Sociology is scientific	Anti-positivist. Rejects sociology as a science
Objective social reality	Subjective social reality
Value free — research free from bias	Value laden — research based on feelings
Discover laws, cause and effect	Gain verstehen (understanding and empathy)
Discover correlations	Uncover meanings
'Top-down' approach	'Bottom-up' approach
Test hypothesis through research	Theory develops from research
Reliability — can replicate	Validity (true picture); insight
Representative — can generalise	Understand individual's 'world view'

Quantitative — numerical data	Qualitative — rich, in-depth data
Structured — standardised questions	Unstructured — no researcher control

PRIMARY METHODS

Survey (census)	Participant observation (PO)
Questionnaire (S. Hite)	Covert (Patrick/Humphries); overt (Barker)
Structured interview (Townsend)	Unstructured interview (Oakley)
Lab experiment (Milgram)	Field experiment (Rosenthal and Jacobsen)

Structured ◄———— Non-PO ————► Unstructured

SECONDARY METHODS

Official statistics (e.g. census data)   Personal documents — diaries, letters, photos

◄———————— Public documents ————————►

Parish records ◄——— Historical data ———► Personal documents
Formal — statistical ◄——— Content analysis ——► Semiology, media messages

Theoretical perspective

Macro — Functionalist and Marxist	Micro — Interactionist
Society influences the individual	Individuals influence society

Figure 1 Two methodological perspectives

Positivism versus interpretivism

- **Positivists** see behaviour as being determined by external forces beyond the individual's control.
- **Interpretivists** argue that individuals make sense of situations during social interactions.
- **Positivists** argue that these external forces, called **social facts**, should be studied scientifically.
- **Interpretivists** argue that sociologists can only study the meanings that individuals give to their behaviour by using **verstehen**.
- **Positivists** use methods that produce quantitative data to examine cause and effect and make laws about human behaviour.
- **Interpretivists** use methods that produce qualitative data in order to understand behaviour from the individual's point of view and gain insight.

Exam tip

In an essay you should state that a particular methodological perspective would *prefer to use* certain methods. Practical or ethical issues could have a greater influence. An interactionist may prefer to use an interpretivist method to study working-class underachievement but the government may only be willing to fund a method that produces quantitative data.

Social facts These are things that exist externally to the individual that they cannot control. This concept was developed by Durkheim (1895) who felt that positivist methods should be used to study social facts like suicide.

Verstehen This refers to understanding social action via placing oneself in someone else's position (empathy). This concept was developed by Max Weber (1922) as a critical response to positivist sociology.

Practical issues

- **Time** Some methods are more time-consuming than others. With covert participant observation, it can often take months for an individual researcher just to gain entry and be accepted by the group studied. In comparison, a self-complete questionnaire can be posted or emailed to respondents by a team of researchers relatively quickly.
- **Cost** Methods using secondary data such as official statistics are often free as these are in the public domain, whereas unstructured interviews are a relatively expensive method due to costs of training interviewers.

  Cost relates to time, as money available affects issues such as how long can be spent on a particular method or sample size. Only the government can afford to conduct a large-scale survey like the census, whereas an individual researcher could conduct a small group interview relatively quickly and cheaply.
- **Funding** Funding bodies such as the government usually require quantitative data in order to gain statistical evidence to measure the impact of educational policies, for example. The sociologist therefore may have no choice but to use methods such as questionnaires or structured interviews. For large-scale research, financial backing from funding bodies is often the most important influence on choice of method.
- **Personal characteristics and skills of the researcher** Some methods such as covert participant observation and unstructured interviews require a great deal of interpersonal skills in order to develop a **rapport** with those studied. Similarly, some researchers may not wish to be involved in the dangerous situations that can arise from covert research. It would also be difficult for a female to conduct a participant observation study on topics such as homosexual activities in male toilets (Humphries) or football hooliganism.
- **Access and opportunity** Access to conduct interviews into organisations like a school can be denied by **gatekeepers** such as head teachers. As a result, a researcher may have to use secondary methods or be restricted to using a postal questionnaire. Barker was invited by the Moonies to study them and so was able to use observation, interviews and questionnaires in her research (**triangulation**).

Rapport A relationship of trust which, if achieved, can lead to a researcher gaining valid data.

> **Exam tip**
>
> In an essay discuss how sociologists may also decide to triangulate and use both types of method. Dobash and Dobash used both structured (to gather statistics on injuries) and unstructured (to gain insight on experiences) interviews in their study of domestic violence.

Triangulation Combining different research methods or sources of data to get a more 'rounded picture' of social reality.

Ethical issues

Sociologists should follow **ethical guidelines** as laid out by the British Sociological Association.

- **Informed consent** Consent is when the participants have agreed to take part in research. In order to gain informed consent the researcher needs to ensure that participants also know the purpose of the research.
- **Right to withdraw** Once they have agreed to take part, participants should be able to drop out at any time.

- **Deception** Covert research involves lying to participants. For example, in covert participant observation, the researcher has to lie to the group in order to gain access.
- **Harm** Researchers must ensure that participants do not suffer any physical or mental harm as a result of the research.
- **Confidentiality** Personal details and identities of participants must remain confidential. For example, if the identities of the men involved in Humphries' study had been revealed it could have had a devastating impact on their lives.

Perhaps the biggest influence on a sociologist's choice of method is their methodological and theoretical perspective. Marxists are more likely to use positivist methods as they help give a large-scale, 'macro' view of patterns of behaviour in society. For Marxists, quantitative data such as statistics from social surveys on poverty will provide evidence of what they would argue are patterns of inequality in a capitalist society. As interactionists are more interested in gaining verstehen, they are more likely to use interpretivist methods to obtain a small-scale, micro view of patterns of behaviour. For example, interactionists will use research methods such as unstructured interviews or observation to examine interaction between teachers and pupils on issues such as teacher labelling. However, practical and ethical factors can also have a major influence on a sociologist's choice of method. These factors may restrict a sociologist's choice of method no matter what their methodological or theoretical perspective is.

Factors that influence choice of topic

Theoretical perspective

The major concerns of different sociological theories will inevitably influence choice of topic. While Marxist sociologists would be interested in studying issues that reflect what they feel are the inevitable consequences of a capitalist system such as income inequality between the classes, feminists would focus on studying the reasons for the pay gap between males and females.

Practical issues

- **Access** Some topics such as corporate crime may be difficult to study due to their secretive nature.
- **Funding** Organisations paying for the research are only going to want to fund research on topics they feel are important. Governments are likely to want to fund research on topics that are of particular interest to them for political reasons.
- **Opportunity** Barker had the unusual opportunity to study a religious cult after being invited by the Moonies to study them.

Exam tip

In an essay, be prepared to discuss how PET (practical, ethical and theoretical) factors are connected. The theoretical advantage of gaining valid data from a method often comes with the practical problems of time and cost. For example, rapport can take a long time to build in covert participant observation or unstructured interviews.

Exam tip

A good form of evaluation is to discuss strategies that a researcher may use to deal with ethical issues such as lack of consent and even harm. If deception is used, sociologists can **debrief** participants on the purpose of the research when it has been completed.

Exam tip

This level of detail on theory is only required for an A-level question.

Contemporary issues

Sociologists, like anyone else, will be influenced by and interested in studying the issues of the day. Sociologists are likely to study topics that are being widely covered in the media at the time.

Exam tip

Many of the issues relating to factors affecting choice of topic (theoretical and practical) are similar to factors that affect choice of method. While exam questions tend to focus on choice of method, make sure you are able to apply these points to choice of topic. For an essay question, you may be asked to look at both!

Summary

After studying this section, you should be able to explain:
- the distinction between primary and secondary data, and between quantitative and qualitative data
- the relationship between positivism, interpretivism and sociological methods; the nature of 'social facts'
- the relationship between sociological theory and methods
- the theoretical, practical and ethical considerations influencing choice of topic, choice of methods and how these are interrelated

Primary research

Conducting a survey

The most common form of gathering data is to conduct a social survey using a self-complete questionnaire or interview. Social surveys have practical advantages as large amounts of quantitative data can be gathered relatively quickly using **pre-coded questions**. Once the sociologist has chosen their topic and acquired funding, various steps need to be undertaken before the research can be conducted. First a research question or aim will need to be formulated, which will narrow the focus of the research. An example of an aim for such a survey might be a study to examine the reasons for differential gender achievement. After establishing an aim, a sociologist may then wish to test a specific **hypothesis**. An example of a hypothesis illustrating the next stage of a survey on gender and achievement might be: 'Gender differences in achievement are the result of differences in teacher attention'.

Before a hypothesis can be tested, concepts need to be operationalised, in other words they must be clearly defined and made measurable. While this is not an issue for gender, 'teacher attention' would need to be operationalised. For example, it could be measured in terms of how often a student was asked a question by a teacher. Finally, before the survey is undertaken, the researcher should conduct a pilot study or 'test run' of the draft questionnaire or **interview schedule** to check whether the questions are clearly understood.

Sampling

For practical reasons sociologists cannot study all of the **research population**, so a sample has to be used.

Pre-coded questions Where each possible response to a question is given a code so that the researcher (for an interview) or respondent (for a self-complete questionnaire) can simply circle the number which corresponds to the chosen answer. This allows data to be quickly analysed via a computer.

Hypothesis A statement which offers an explanation which is tested.

Interview schedule A list of the interview questions.

Research population The whole group the researcher is interested in studying.

Representative sampling

Sociologists, particularly positivists, will usually use a sample that is representative and reflects a cross section of the research population in order that they can generalise their findings. In the above example of gender and achievement, the research population is the 1,000 pupils at a school and the researcher could use the following techniques to obtain the desired sample of 100.

- **Simple random sampling** This is where everyone has an equal chance of being selected. In the example, the sample would be the first 100 student names drawn out of a hat.

- **Systematic random sampling** This involves picking every 'nth' number from a sampling frame, which is a list of names of those in the research population. In the example, this would mean picking every tenth pupil from the school's roll. As with random sampling, it is unlikely that the sample produced would be representative (e.g. that 50 females and 50 males would be selected).

- **Stratified random sampling** This involves dividing the research population into specific groups and making a random selection with the right proportions. If the researcher stratified by age and gender in the school survey, it would mean that ten males and ten females from Years 7 to 11 would be randomly selected from these two categories to make up the sample of 100.

- **Quota sampling** This involves the researcher picking people for the sample who fit a certain category. This is non-random as the researcher chooses each person but, like stratified random sampling, it can lead to a representative sample. In the example, the researcher could decide to have a quota of two males and two females from ethnic minority backgrounds for the ten students in each year group (if this was proportional to the population of the school).

Non-representative sampling methods

Sociologists, however, particularly interpretivists, may not be interested in generalising and so may use a non-representative sample.

There may also be practical reasons why a representative sample cannot be obtained. For example, there is no sampling frame for criminals, who are also likely to refuse to take part in a survey. For such groups **snowball sampling** can be used when an initial contact researched gives more names for the sample. For example, one criminal would put the researcher in contact with two more criminals and so the sample would increase (snowball).

Opportunity sampling such as interviewing people in a shopping centre may be practical but is also not intended to be representative.

For the following sociological research methods, WWWE (**W**hat, **W**ho, **W**hy and Evaluation) is used to define and outline their major strengths and weaknesses. The first evaluation point refers to why positivists or interpretivists would not use the method. Where subsequent points are numbered, strengths (+) of the method have been related to weaknesses (−). Other evaluation points or tables may follow.

Questionnaires

What A questionnaire is a list of standardised questions, usually closed, with pre-coded answers. Self-complete questionnaires are usually sent to respondents'

Knowledge check 12

Outline two types of random sampling techniques.

Exam tip

WWWE can be used as a template for your introduction (see page 45). In essays you should try to link strengths of a method to weaknesses based on practical, ethical and theoretical issues (PET). You should also use examples and studies to develop AO2 and AO3.

homes and returned by post or email but can be distributed in person such as in a classroom. If a questionnaire is read out to a respondent this becomes a structured interview (see page 00).

Who and **Why** Positivists would tend to use questionnaires as, due to their standardised nature, they are reliable and provide quantitative data which can be used to establish correlations and test a hypothesis.

Evaluation

However, interpretivists would reject questionnaires as they do not give a true picture of respondents' meanings and so lack validity.

1. + They can be distributed to a large, geographically spread (P) and representative sample (T).
   − They may be seen as 'junk mail' or 'spam' and only certain people may return them, leading to a low response rate (P) and potentially an unrepresentative sample (T).

2. + They are quick and cheap (P).
   − They may take a long time to be returned and an incentive (such as a free pen) may be needed to get the respondent to fill in and complete, which will add to the cost (P).

3. + As they are self-complete, there are no interviewer costs (P) or interviewer bias (T).
   − There is no control for the researcher; the respondent may not receive the questionnaire or the wrong person may fill it in. The questions cannot be explained (P).

4. + Closed, pre-coded questions are easy to analyse via computer programs so patterns and correlations can be identified (P).
   − The imposition problem may undermine validity (T) as respondents may not be able to express their true feelings in closed questions (P).

5. + Detachment: positivists favour questionnaires as they are objective — there is no personal contact between the researcher and the respondent (T).
   − Detachment: interpretivists reject questionnaires as a lack of contact leads to a lack of verstehen — meanings cannot be clarified by the researcher (T).

6. + There are relatively few ethical issues due to the lack of contact (E).
   − A researcher still needs to gain informed consent, ensure anonymity and not use questions that may lead to harm (E).

Studies

- **Shere Hite** (1991). This study illustrates that questionnaires may not be appropriate for studying certain topics, in this case women's sexual health. As the questions related to sensitive and personal issues, there was a low response rate (4.5%) meaning that findings could not be generalised due to the sample being unrepresentative. Only certain types of women may have responded.
- **Bowles and Gintis** (1976). Bowles and Gintis gave 237 questionnaires to New York high school students to gain information on the character traits that were

Interviewer bias Where an interviewer affects the respondent's answers and thereby reduces validity, e.g. through tone of voice, facial expressions or, particularly in unstructured interviews, leading questions.

Imposition problem Where a researcher 'forces' the respondent to answer in a certain way; e.g. with closed questions and pre-coded responses, the researcher has already decided what questions are important and how people can respond.

rewarded by schools and employers. They used a reasonably large sample so that they could generalise their findings and support their hypothesis that the correspondence principle existed between schools and the workplace.

Knowledge check 13

Outline two theoretical strengths of using questionnaires.

Structured interviews

What A structured interview is when a questionnaire (a list of standardised questions, usually closed, with pre-coded answers) is read out to respondents and filled in by a trained interviewer.

Who and **Why** Positivists would tend to use structured interviews as, due to their standardised nature, they are reliable. They provide quantitative data which can be used to establish correlations and test a hypothesis.

Evaluation

However, interpretivists reject structured interviews as they do not give a true picture of respondents' meanings and so lack validity.

As structured interviews share the main strengths and weaknesses of questionnaires, the relative advantages and disadvantages between the two methods are examined (see table).

Advantages	Disadvantages
Higher response rate as respondents find it harder to turn down a researcher if face to face (P)	They are more expensive due to interviewer costs and cannot have as geographically dispersed and as large samples (P)
It is more difficult for a respondent to lie face to face so potentially data are more valid (T)	Respondents are more likely to give socially desirable answers due to the 'halo effect' (T)
Interviewers can clarify questions, although they may have strict guidelines to follow (T)	Interviewer bias may undermine validity (T)

Table 7 Advantages and disadvantages of structured interviews compared to questionnaires

Studies

- **Young and Willmott** (1962). This study used structured interviews to gather large amounts of factual data about family life in London. The study also illustrates the practical advantages of having a large sample (987 people) and having a high response rate (94%).
- **Peter Townsend** (1979). This study used structured interviews to administer a 39-page questionnaire on poverty in the UK. As well having a high response rate (76%) to a large sample, interviewers were required to administer pre-coded questions on household income that were often very complex.

Unstructured interviews

What An unstructured interview is an informal conversation between an interviewer and a respondent which has no set format.

Who and **Why** Interpretivists would tend to use unstructured interviews as they enable respondents to discuss issues from their point of view, therefore gaining verstehen and valid data.

Evaluation

However, positivists reject unstructured interviews as they are non-standardised and so data gained will lack reliability. As samples are usually small, they are likely to be unrepresentative.

1. + The freedom of having no structure and open questions allows the researcher to follow up leads (P).
   - They can be time-consuming and expensive. Responses will be difficult to quantify and may be irrelevant (P).

2. + If a rapport is developed, valid data can be obtained on sensitive topics (T).
   - This will only occur if the researcher is highly skilled (P), and rapport may lead to socially desirable responses (T).

3. + They enable the researcher to uncover the meanings behind the respondent's actions without the imposition problem (T).
   - The problem of interview bias is greater than with structured interviews, for example interviewers may only follow up leads they feel are important (T).

4. + There are relatively few ethical issues (E).
   - The interviewee may feel under pressure to answer questions that are personal. The right to withdraw and anonymity must be ensured (E).

Interviews can also be **semi-structured**, which is when there are some structured, more standardised questions but the interviewer is allowed the flexibility to follow up areas of interest.

Sociologists can also conduct **group interviews** with respondents, who are sometimes called focus groups. The advantages of these are that groups, such as students, may be more relaxed and can 'bounce' ideas from one another, leading to more valid data. However, there is the problem that one member of the group may dominate the discussion and peer pressure may affect the validity of responses.

Interpretivists prefer these methods as valid data can be obtained. However, positivists would argue that their non-standardised nature leads to a lack of reliability.

Studies

- **Dobash and Dobash** (1980). Dobash and Dobash conducted 109 unstructured interviews with women who had been the victims of domestic violence. This study illustrates that to help gain rapport on this very sensitive issue the interviews were conducted informally in the refuges where the women lived. The interviews gained valid data but raised practical problems as they took between 2 and 12 hours.
- **Ann Oakley** (1973). Oakley interviewed 66 women during and after pregnancy. The study illustrates that if the interviewer gains empathy and rapport with the interviewees they will feel comfortable discussing personal subjects. A theoretical problem may have been that Oakley may have become too attached to the women so the data may have lacked validity.

Participant observation (PO)

What Where the researcher joins in with the activities of the group being studied. This can be either **covert**, where the researcher goes 'undercover' ('closed') or **overt**, where the researcher's true identity is made known ('open').

> **Exam tip**
> Be prepared to relate methods to theory. For example, feminists are in favour of unstructured interviews as they allow women to be more in control of the research process.

> **Focus groups** An informal group interview where a researcher introduces a topic and allows the group to tease out responses from one another.

Who and **Why** Interpretivists would tend to use participant observation as it gives a first-hand insight into the social interactions and behaviour of the group studied.

Evaluation

However, positivists would reject PO due to its lack of reliability as it cannot be standardised or replicated. Tables 8, 9 and 10 constitute a 'revision chart' for PO that could be used for other methods.

Strengths	Weaknesses
Can observe people in their natural setting and gain valid data (T)	Can only observe small groups, so cannot generalise findings (P)
Subjective involvement means insight and verstehen can be gained (T)	Positivists argue that PO is not scientific. As it is based on one researcher's interpretation it cannot be replicated (T)
Can study behaviour of groups over time (P)	PO can be time-consuming and expensive (P)

Table 8 Strengths and weaknesses of both covert and overt PO

Overt	Covert
Honest method as there is no deception (E)	Lack of informed consent (E)
Hawthorne effect means data may lack validity. Behaviour will change if participants know they are being observed (T)	Hawthorne effect does not occur but the presence of the researcher may still affect the group dynamics (T)
Can ask naive but important questions and use other methods openly (P)	Asking such questions may blow the researcher's cover (P)
Easy to record information (P)	Will have to record information later (P) and rely on memory, which may affect validity (T)
Researcher does not have to take part in all the group's activities as they are not 'one of them' (P) (E)	Researcher may have to take part in activities they disagree with or break the law (P) (E)

Table 9 Comparison of covert and overt PO

Getting in Hard to gain access, particularly with deviant groups	With overt, the group may deny access or stop the researcher from seeing everything. With covert, it may be hard for an 'outsider' to gain the trust of the group
Staying in Researcher may 'go native' and get too involved	More likely with covert as the researcher takes part in all the group's activities
Getting out Leaving the group may be difficult	Less of a problem for overt as the researcher is not pretending to be part of the group

Table 10 Covert and overt PO in relation to 'getting in, staying in and getting out'

When conducting participant observation, sociologists sometimes fall between being covert and overt. Studies such as Patrick can be described as **semi-overt** as a key member of the group, such as a gang leader, is told the real purpose of the study. William Foote Whyte (1938) told the gang that the reason for joining was that he needed information for a book he was writing about their neighbourhood. Only the gang leader was told it was actually the gang itself he was studying.

Although less common, sociologists can also use covert and overt non-participant observation. Interpretivists would tend not to use this method as they would argue that a lack of participation in the activities of the group reduces the level of verstehen and therefore validity. While positivists totally reject participant observation, they may occasionally use non-participant observation using a **structured observation schedule**. For example, in a lesson observation the frequency of interactions between teachers and pupils could be quantified and used to establish correlations.

Studies

- **James Patrick** (1973). Patrick's **covert** study of a Glasgow gang can be used to illustrate the issue of 'getting in' as he was close to the boys' age and gained access through the gang leader 'Tim'. 'Getting out' was a problem for Patrick as he had to leave the gang abruptly due to the violence. Due to fear of repercussions, he published his study years later under a false name.
- **Laud Humphries** (1970). Humphries' initially **covert** study of gay sexual activities in public toilets in the USA can be used to illustrate the issue of 'getting in' in terms of the observer's role. Humphries acted as a 'watch queen' (lookout) as part of the process of gaining the trust of this very secretive group who were engaging in illegal behaviour. Once he had gained their trust, Humphries revealed the purpose of his research to certain participants (became **overt**), which allowed him use other methods such as interviews.
- **Maurice Punch** (1979). Punch's **overt** study of Amsterdam police can be used to illustrate the problem of 'getting in' as the police officers only let Punch see certain aspects of their activities on patrol. It also shows the issue of 'staying in' in terms of going native as he starting behaving like a police officer and chased suspects.
- **Eileen Barker** (1984). Barker's **case study** on a religious sect (the Moonies) and whether they were 'brainwashing' their members can be used to illustrate how a researcher conducting **overt** participant observation can become a 'trusted outsider'. While initially her observations may have lacked validity due to the Hawthorne effect, Barker was with the Moonies for 6 years and was able to build up rapport with group members. Barker may have 'gone native', however, and have become too sympathetic to the Moonies as a result, thus compromising the validity of her findings. Was Barker herself brainwashed by the Moonies?

Exam tip

If a question asks you to evaluate the problems of using covert or overt participant observation, be prepared to use non-participant observation as evaluation to compare the relative strengths and weaknesses of the methods.

Laboratory experiments

What A laboratory experiment is a test carried out in a controlled environment to establish cause and effect between identified variables. The researcher changes the independent variable to measure the effect on the dependent variable.

Who and **Why** Positivists tend to use laboratory experiments as, due to their high levels of reliability, they are easy to replicate.

Structured observation schedule A pre-defined list of behaviour patterns that a researcher is investigating.

Case study A detailed study of one group or event usually involving a variety of qualitative methods. Barker used overt observation, questionnaires and unstructured interviews in her study on the Moonies. While interpretivists favour case studies due to valid data being gained, positivists would reject their use as the findings cannot be generalised.

Knowledge check 14

Outline two ethical problems of using covert participant observation.

Evaluation

However, interpretivists reject their use as they lack ecological validity due to the fact that they take place in an artificial environment.

1 + As the researcher has control over the experiment (P), the data should be reliable (T).
   – The variables that influence human behaviour cannot easily be identified or controlled (P).
2 + Behaviour patterns can be measured quantitatively via manipulating variables (P).
   – The Hawthorne effect and **experimenter effect** could influence the behaviour of the participant rather than the independent variable (T).

Other problems:
■ Ethical issues — laboratory experiments often involve deception as to the true purpose of the experiment and may cause emotional and physical harm to the participants (E).
■ They cannot be used to study the past (P).
■ They are not representative (T) due to their small scale (P).

Studies
■ **Stanley Milgram** (1974). In this 'shocking' study, participants were misled into thinking that they were administering potentially fatal electric shocks to people when they answered a question incorrectly. Despite the ethical problems of deception, physical harm (some had seizures) and emotional harm, (knowing that they could have killed because they were told to), Milgram's study illustrates how 'the end justifies the means'. In the debrief, 74% of participants felt they had learned something on Milgram's topic of obedience and authority, despite being deceived.
■ **Albert Bandura** (1961). Bandura's experiment on the influence of the media on violent behaviour can be used to illustrate the ethical issues of whether children can give their full informed consent and the potential harm caused by the researcher exposing them to violence.

Field experiments

What A field experiment is a test carried out in a natural environment to establish cause and effect between identified variables.

Who and **Why** Interpretivists tend to use field experiments as they can uncover hidden meanings in a natural environment.

Evaluation

However, positivists would reject them as they are more difficult to replicate and so lack reliability.

1 + As the research takes place in the participant's natural surroundings, the data will be more valid (T).
   – Variables cannot easily be controlled as is the case in a laboratory (P).
2 + As the participants are usually unaware that they are in an experiment, there is no Hawthorne effect (T).
   – This creates problems of lack of informed consent and deception, which may lead to harm (E).

Experimenter effect
When the behaviour of a participant is influenced by the very fact of them being aware that they are involved in an experiment.

Exam tip
In an essay, develop analysis by stating that due to these problems even positivists are very unlikely to use laboratory experiments despite their high reliability.

Knowledge check 15
Outline two practical problems of using laboratory experiments.

Exam tip
A common error made by students is to confuse field experiments with participant observation. While they may both involve studying a group in their natural environment, in a field experiment the researcher does not participate in the behaviour of the group.

Studies

- **Rosenthal and Jacobsen** (1968). Rosenthal and Jacobsen conducted a field experiment to test their theory on the self-fulfilling prophecy and the impact of teacher labelling. This study can be used to illustrate the problem of identifying and controlling variables. There may have been factors other than the variable of teacher expectations that influenced the improvements in the IQ of the students. It also illustrates ethical problems of deception as the teachers were lied to and potential harm in relation to the possible impact on the students' education.
- **Mary Sissons** (1971). Sissons' study on the effect of social class on people's willingness to give directions to an actor (who dressed as a businessman then a labourer outside Paddington train station) can be used to show the problem of lack of reliability. It would be impossible to have exactly the same members of the public involved, so the study cannot be replicated.

Secondary research

Official statistics

What Official statistics are quantitative data gathered and used by the government and other official bodies.

Who and Why Positivists would tend to use official statistics as they are reliable and they can be used to identify correlations to test a hypothesis.

> **Exam tip**
>
> In an essay question, you can develop AO2 and AO3 despite there being no ethical weaknesses of official statistics. Compare the ethical strengths of official statistics (e.g. they are secondary data that do not require consent) with other methods such as covert participant observation, which has ethical issues such as deception and potential harm to both the researcher and the group.

Evaluation

However, interpretivists reject official statistics as they lack validity.

Strengths	Weaknesses
Often the only source of data in a particular area, e.g. the census (P)	Collected by the government so may not be on the topic researched (P)
Free source of large amounts of quantitative data; in the public domain and easily accessible online (P)	They are secondary data and not collected by sociologists themselves, so there is no control over collection (P)
Data are reliable as they are compiled in a standardised way by 'experts', e.g. the census (T)	Not always fully reliable, e.g. mistakes could be made when data are recorded onto or from census forms (T)
Hard statistics allow accurate comparisons between groups. For example, we can compare statistics on social class and divorce rates (T)	Soft statistics may not be very valid as they do not always measure what they are supposed to. For example, the police do not record all crimes (T)
Shows trends and patterns over time as they are often collected at regular intervals. For example, can compare the rise in female achievement after policies like GIST (P). Could be used to test a hypothesis (T)	How data are collected may change over time, e.g. unemployment statistics. Thatcher's government changed definitions over 20 times in 1980s (P). Marxists would argue they are manipulated by the government for political reasons (T)
Positivists argue that the quantitative data enable sociologists to identify and accurately measure behaviour patterns and establish cause and effect relationships (T)	Interpretivists would argue that official statistics are socially constructed, 'made up by society'. For example, crime statistics tell us more about police labelling than levels of crime (T)
Usually large scale and are therefore representative. For example, the census covers the whole population as it is compulsory (T)	Some may not be as representative, as they are only based on a sample of the relevant population, e.g. the Crime Survey for England and Wales (T)
No ethical issues (E)	

Table 11 Strengths and weaknesses of using official statistics

Studies

- **Durkheim** (1897). Durkheim used **the comparative method** to compare different suicide rates (official statistics) of different European countries. As a positivist, Durkheim felt that he was able to use a scientific approach to prove his hypothesis that the more integrated into society a person was the less likely they would be to commit suicide.
- **The Crime Survey of England and Wales**. Formally the British Crime Survey, this is a systematic victim survey that provides crime statistics based on a sample of up to 50,000 people. Positivist researchers would use statistics from this survey to examine patterns and trends in crime.

Documents

What Documents refer to a wide range of written and other 'texts' that can be personal (such as letters, photo albums and autobiographies) and public (such as government reports).

Who and Why Interpretivists would tend to use them, particularly personal, expressive documents such as diaries, as they can be used to uncover meanings and are a rich source of qualitative data.

Evaluation

Positivists tend not use documents as they lack reliability due to their unstandardised nature. However, positivists may use formal documents such as parish records which contain quantitative data that could be used to establish correlations.

1   + As they are secondary data, documents are often free, quick and easy to collect (P).
   – They may not be specifically on the topic required and some documents may be difficult to access. There may be legal restrictions to the use of some public documents (P).
2   + As they are secondary, there are limited ethical issues (E).
   – Some documents such as diaries will need consent (E).
3   + Personal documents such as diaries are not written with an audience in mind, so can provide a valid and authentic picture of the writer's thoughts and feelings (T).
   – Personal documents may lack validity. For example, diaries may exaggerate personal experiences while autobiographies are likely to be biased towards the writer's view (T).
4   + Historical documents are sometimes the only way of studying the past (P).
   – There may be no way of checking the validity of the original research (P) (T).

Sociologists may use **content analysis** to systematically study the content of documents, particularly the media. Formal content analysis is favoured by positivists to count the frequency of pre-determined categories such as male or female voiceovers in adverts. Interpretivists would prefer to use **semiotic** content analysis, which involves examining the themes and underlying meanings in documents such as the wording used in news reporting. While there are practical advantages of easy access and low

The comparative method A 'thought experiment' conducted in the mind of a sociologist.

Knowledge check 16

What is the difference between hard and soft official statistics?

Exam tip

Be prepared to apply John Scott's (1990) checklist when assessing documents' authenticity (is it fake?), credibility (is it believable?), representativeness (is it typical?) and meaning (is it understandable?).

cost to media sources, there are problems with content analysis. **Formal** content analysis would be rejected by interpretivists for not examining the meanings behind the frequency, while positivists would reject more qualitative content analysis for being subjective as it is based on the researcher's interpretation of the media message.

Studies

- **Thomas and Znaniecki** (1919). This classic study on Polish immigrants to the USA can be used to show the high levels of meaning that documents can provide the researcher. Thomas and Znaniecki used a wide range of private documents such as letters sent home and public documents such as newspaper articles.
- **The Glasgow University Media Group**. The GUMG has conducted a wide variety of content analysis studies since the 1970s on a range of issues. These studies have been useful to illustrate the biased nature of news reporting. They arguably also show that bias can occur in relation to the interpretation of media sources when conducting content analysis.

Knowledge check 17

Outline two practical strengths of using documents.

Summary

After studying this section, you should be able to explain:
- the stages a sociologist follows when conducting a survey, including sampling techniques
- sources of data, including questionnaires, interviews, participant and non-participant observation, experiments, documents and official statistics
- the distinction between primary and secondary data, and between quantitative and qualitative data

■ Sociological theory and methods (A-level only)

Sociological theory

- Functionalism is a consensus theory which argues that society is based on shared values.
- Marxism is a conflict theory which argues that we live in a capitalist society in which there is a relationship based on conflict, with the bourgeoisie (the 'bosses') exploiting the proletariat (the 'workers').
- Both functionalism and Marxism are 'macro', large-scale theories that tend to use positivist methods. These approaches are referred to as structural theories as society is seen as shaping individuals' behaviour.
- Social action theories reject structural, macro theories and argue that society is constructed through people's interactions and meanings (such as in the labelling process).
- Social action theories such as interactionism are 'micro', small-scale theories that tend to use interpretivist methods. Some neo-Marxists such as Willis have incorporated social action theory and interpretivist methods into their research.
- Feminists argue that other sociological theories are 'malestream', as they largely ignore the issues of patriarchy and gender inequality in society. Feminists mainly use interpretivist methods to study issues such as the division of domestic labour and domestic violence.

Exam tip

For A-level Paper 1 you only have a 10-mark question on this area (it can also be on sociological methods). For this question you only need to look at two points, for example two arguments for or against a claim such as sociology being a science, or two advantages or disadvantages of a method. Refer to Student Guide 3 for a more detailed coverage of this topic.

- Liberal feminists argue that changes in legislation such as the Equal Pay Act are gradually leading to greater equality for women. However, radical feminists argue that society is based on the oppression of women and that only revolutionary change will bring about an end to the gender inequality that results from patriarchy.
- Postmodernists argue that 'modern' theories such as functionalism and Marxism are 'grand narratives' ('big stories') that do not hold the 'truth' about society. They are out of date as they are no longer able to explain the diverse and fragmented nature of postmodern society.
- Theories of late modernity agree with postmodernism that society has changed rapidly in recent years but argue that we are still in the modern era.

Sociology, science and value freedom

- Positivists such as Durkheim argue that sociology can and should model itself on the natural sciences and use quantitative methods to study society objectively.
- Positivists argue that sociologists can discover laws about human behaviour by using the inductive method where data is gathered through observation and measurement. The process of verification should be used to prove or refute a hypothesis.
- Positivists believe that as sociologists can study social phenomena objectively, value freedom is possible as the researcher's own beliefs will not influence how they conduct their research or interpret their results.
- Popper rejected the inductive approach of positivism and argued that scientific knowledge should be based on the process of falsification (that it can be proved wrong) rather than verification. Popper felt that while sociology could be scientific as it can produce a hypothesis that can be tested, most sociology is unscientific as it cannot be proved wrong.
- Kuhn argues that as sociology does not have a shared **paradigm** it cannot be considered to be a science.
- Realists argue that like some natural scientists, such as meteorologists, sociologists have to study society in 'open systems' where variables cannot necessarily be controlled and measured. Therefore realists argue that although sociology can attempt to be scientific in studying open systems in a neutral way it cannot be completely value free.
- Interpretivists and social action theorists reject the claim that sociology can be an objective science. They argue that the purpose of sociological inquiry is to uncover meanings and gain verstehen through qualitative methods, not to establish cause and effect. Rather than being value free and objective, they would argue that sociologists need to be subjective and will inevitably be influenced by their values.
- Weber argued the sociologists could not be value free when choosing a research topic and interpreting and applying findings. However, he felt that researchers must be objective and unbiased when carrying out their research.
- Some sociologists, such as Marxists and feminists, argue that value freedom is undesirable and that sociologists should be value laden; they should make value judgements and should aim to improve society through sociological research.

> **Knowledge check 18**
>
> Outline two qualitative research methods that Willis used to study the 'lads'.

> **Paradigm** An assumed way of looking at the world, for example the Earth is flat.

> **Knowledge check 19**
>
> What is the difference between verification and falsification?

Sociology and social policy

Social policies are parts of government policies that attempt to deal with social problems such as educational underachievement, poverty and crime. Social policy has been influenced by sociological perspectives and research in a variety of ways.

■ The social democratic perspective had a significant impact on the introduction of the welfare state after the Second World War. Later, Townsend's *Poverty in the United Kingdom* made recommendations to the government to change what he felt was an inadequate benefits system.

■ New Right researchers such as Marsland and his notion of the dependency culture influenced the Conservative governments to cut back on welfare provision in the 1980s. The New Right believe that the state should have a minimal role in people's lives and therefore they criticise most social policy.

■ Feminist theory and research has influenced government policies aimed at addressing gender inequality, such as GIST and the Equal Pay Act.

■ Many Marxists are critical of government social policies and argue that they can be used by the capitalist system to maintain and justify inequality. For example, they would argue that the minimum wage legitimises exploitation in the labour market while giving the impression to the public that governments are acting in the best interests of the low paid. While some Marxists acknowledge that some social policies have benefited the working class, their main function is to pacify the proletariat to ensure that they do not rebel.

■ Some sociologists believe that their research should feed into social policy. Functionalists would argue that sociologists should provide the state with scientific, objective information on which the state can base its policies.

■ Others, such as 'modern positivists', feel that it is the job of sociologists to find out what is happening with social problems, but that it is up to someone else to solve them.

■ Despite the influence of sociological research on social policy, governments may reject findings for a variety of reasons such as cost and their political standpoint.

> **Knowledge check 20**
>
> Outline three educational policies that have been influenced by the New Right.

Summary

After studying this section, you should be aware of:
■ consensus, conflict, structural and social action theories
■ the concepts of modernity and postmodernity in relation to sociological theory
■ the relationship between theory and methods
■ the nature of science and the extent to which sociology can be regarded as scientific
■ debates about subjectivity, objectivity and value freedom
■ the relationship between sociology and social policy

Questions & Answers

■ How to use this section

After this introduction, this section of the guide contains four test papers on **Education, Sociological Methods and Theory** in the style of the questions you can expect in the AS Paper 1 and Paper 2 Section A examinations and in the A-level Paper 1 examination. The content, timings and mark allocation of these papers are shown below.

Each question is followed by a brief analysis of what to watch out for when answering it (shown by the icon ⓔ). The first three papers include an A-grade response (Candidate A) and a C-grade response (Candidate B) to each question, with commentary (preceded by the icon ⓔ). The A-grade responses represent one way of achieving an A grade. However, there is no such thing as a perfect essay. An A grade can be achieved in a number of different ways. The advice below offers some suggestions on how this can be achieved. A fourth paper contains AS and A-level papers for you to try yourself after reading the advice.

AS Papers 1 and 2

Paper 1 Education with methods in context

The exam paper is allocated 1 hour 30 minutes.

- **Education** Short answers (two 2-mark questions and one 6-mark question) and extended writing (10- and 20-mark questions). 40 marks
- **Methods in context** one extended writing question. 20 marks

Paper 2 Research methods and topics in sociology

The exam paper is allocated 1 hour 30 minutes.

- **Section A Research methods** Short answers (4 marks) and extended writing (16 marks). 20 marks
- **Section B Topics in sociology** Short answers and extended writing account for 40 marks. (Section B is not covered in this book.)

A-level

Paper 1 Education with theory and methods

The exam paper is allocated 2 hours.

- **Education** Short answers (4- and 6-mark questions) and extended writing (10- and 30-mark questions). 50 marks
- **Methods in context** One extended writing question. 20 marks
- **Theory and methods** Extended writing. 10 marks

> **Exam tip**
>
> Most of the extended writing questions will make a specific reference to an 'item'. You should always make use of the item but should never copy out material from it. Try to refer to it and use it to make your own point in your own words.

Essay-writing templates

While there is no set way of writing an essay, the following templates can be used to answer the extended writing questions in both the AS and A-level exams. These templates are referred to in the commentary on the sample answers in this section.

Template 1: AS Paper 2 (Section A) Research methods essay

In the AS Paper 2 Section A you will be required to answer a 16-mark question on sociological methods. If the question is evaluating the problems or strengths of a particular method, the following template could be used.

Introduction — WWWE
- **W**hat — define the method
- **W**ho — would generally use it?
- **W**hy — would they use it?
- **E**valuation — who would not use the method and, briefly, why?

If, for example, you refer to the positivist and interpretivist views of the method in the introduction, you have already begun to address one of the key aspects of an A-grade answer: a strong theoretical context.

Main body — practical, ethical and theoretical (PET) paragraphs

For the main body of your essay, base your paragraphs around PET.

For each paragraph, develop AO2 and AO3 by using the following techniques:
- Use studies and examples to illustrate strengths and weaknesses of the method.
- Compare relative strengths and weaknesses with other methods.
- Link strengths of a method to weaknesses.

Conclusion
1 Suggest the major strength and/or weakness of the method and say why.
2 Refer to which topic(s) the method is useful or not useful for studying.
3 Try to say something 'new' and refer to methodological perspectives.

In your conclusion, do not just recap what you have already written as this will add nothing to your essay. Also, try to avoid using 'catch all' points such as 'sociologists should triangulate and use different methods'. This is likely to add little as it does not focus on the method outlined in the question.

> **Exam tip**
>
> A good revision strategy is to practise writing essay questions under exam conditions. Use these plans to help prepare writing 'methods' essay questions. You could use the template to construct your own more detailed plan for each method.

The following notes for a response to an exam-style question from AS Paper 2 illustrate use of the template. You can attempt to write this question using the template under exam conditions. Allow yourself approximately 25 minutes.

Question 02

Evaluate the problems of using self-complete questionnaires when conducting research. (16 marks)

> **Introduction**
>
> Self-complete questionnaires are a list of standardised questions that are given to a respondent to complete on their own. Positivists tend to use them as they generate reliable, quantitative data that can be used to test a hypothesis. However, interpretivists would not use them as they lack validity.
>
> **Main body**
>
> Paragraphs 1 and 2. Practical strengths and weaknesses. Use AO2 and AO3 strategies.
>
> Paragraphs 3 and 4. Theoretical strengths and weaknesses. Use AO2 and AO3 strategies.
>
> Paragraphs 5 and 6. Ethical strengths and weaknesses. Use AO2 and AO3 strategies.

(e) Depending on the method, you may not need two paragraphs on P, E and T. For example, as questionnaires have relatively few ethical issues, one paragraph should suffice. Conversely, you would need at least two paragraphs on ethics for covert participant observation.

(e) Aim to link different PET issues such as a practical problem leading to a theoretical problem, e.g. low response rate (P) means the sample may not be representative so findings cannot be generalised (T).

> **Conclusion**
>
> Perhaps the main strength of self-complete questionnaires is the theoretical/ practical/ethical issue of ...
>
> Perhaps the main weakness of self-complete questionnaires is the theoretical/ practical/ethical issue of ...
>
> As S. Hite's study shows, questionnaires may not be useful for studying sensitive topics because ...
>
> This is why interpretivists reject their use as they would argue that unstructured interviews would be a more effective method to use because ...

Template 2: AS and A-level Paper 1 Education essay

The following template could be used to construct your own more detailed plan for the **item-based essay questions**. For AS this is question 05 in Paper 1 and is worth 20 marks. For A- level it is question 04 in Paper 1 and is worth 30 marks.

Introduction — AAA

- **A** — 'As Item A states ...'
- **A** — Argument 1 — For example, internal factors such as ... (in a question on achievement)
- **A** — Argument 2 — However, also external factors such as ...

Main body

Paragraphs 1–3 on Argument 1 — Include AO2 and AO3 points in each paragraph.

For each paragraph, develop AO2 and AO3 by using the following techniques:
- Use studies and examples to illustrate strengths and weaknesses of the argument.
- Give specific evaluation points on arguments such as supporting evidence being out of date or that it cannot be generalised easily.
- Give evaluation points from different sociological arguments.

Paragraph 4 on Argument 2 — State how it disagrees/agrees with Argument 1.

Paragraph 5 on other possible arguments — State how they disagree/agree with Argument 1.

Conclusion

'Perhaps the main strength of Argument 1 is that it is right to point to the importance of ...'

'Perhaps the main weakness of Argument 1, as Argument 2 points out, is that it ignores the impact of ...'

Say 'something new'. Try not to just recap previous points in the conclusion.

The main body of this template is useful for a question that focuses on a particular argument. You must clearly apply other arguments as to how they agree or disagree with it. If the question requires you to assess sociological explanations of an issue, such as the role of education, you should allocate time more equally to the main arguments.

Depending on the issue raised in the question, the number of paragraphs you devote to each argument will vary. As stated, you should not wait until paragraph 4 to use other theories to evaluate; this should be done throughout the essay.

Methods in context question: applying your knowledge and understanding of sociological research methods to the study of a particular issue in education

In both the AS (Paper 1 question 06) and A-level (Paper 1 question 05) exam, you will have a 20-mark question in which you must apply sociological research methods to the study of education. This question can be broken down into different levels of response.

Level 0 (L0) — topic-only response

This response just discusses the topic raised in the question and on its own is unlikely to achieve more than a U grade.

Level 1 (L1) — methods-only response

A major failing of students' responses to this question is answering it as 'methods-only' question (as in Paper 2 Section A of the AS exam). Even if this type of answer presents an excellent coverage of the strengths and limitations of the method, this response is unlikely to achieve more than a D grade.

In your introduction, remember to use WWWE on the method (see Template 1). If you mention why positivists/interpretivists use/do not use the method you will be able to get maximum possible marks for L1.

Level 2 (L2) — application

Below are some general Level 2 application issues relating either to research characteristics of studying groups involved in education (pupils, teachers and parents) or to the context of studying in an educational institution such as a school. You will be able to refer to some of these issues regardless of the topic raised in the question. Responses that have good Level 1 and have a range of developed Level 2 application can achieve up to a B grade, without even referring to the particular issue raised in the question.

To develop your AO2 marks, make sure you relate these points to PET and apply them specifically to the method referred to in the question.

You should apply ethical issues relating to the context of studying schools to different methods. For example, in terms of the ethical issue of students missing out on curriculum time, it may be easier for a sociologist to persuade a head teacher to allow them to give out a brief questionnaire to students in a tutor period as opposed to withdrawing students for a lengthy unstructured interview in a core subject like maths.

Pupils

Theoretical issues can be explained in terms of the problem of the researcher being seen as a 'teacher in disguise' by the pupil so that data may lack validity. For example, pupils may be reluctant to discuss their true feelings on teacher labelling or parental support in an interview as they may be afraid that this will get back to teachers or their parents. They may give socially desirable answers as they do not want to be put in a detention or be grounded! The language used in primary methods such as questionnaires and interviews will need to be kept simple and 'student friendly' in order to obtain valid data. For example, younger students may have problems understanding complex questions and sociological concepts such as cultural deprivation. For the Hawthorne effect and observations of lessons students could either behave better than usual to get on their teacher's 'good side' or be more disruptive so they can get a teacher they dislike into 'trouble'. Develop points by comparing how different students may prefer different types of methods. An interview may be easier than a self-complete questionnaire for a student with learning difficulties so that more valid data is obtained. Practical issues such as the questionnaires being too long may mean that pupils get bored or do not want to fill them in if they have to be completed out of lesson time. In terms of ethical issues, pupils are a vulnerable group so as well as needing parental consent there is the issue of whether they are mature enough to give informed consent. Will Year 5 pupils really understand the purpose of the research even if it is explained to them? Sociologists will also need to be mindful of causing harm such as the potential negative impact on pupils' education. For example, pupils involved in an interview are likely to be missing out on lesson time at the very least.

Teachers

In a similar way, teachers may see the researcher as 'Ofsted in disguise' so this raises the theoretical problem that responses may lack validity. Teachers may be afraid of losing their job if they give honest answers in interviews or questionnaires on issues such as racism in schools. Again, with lesson observations explain how the Hawthorne effect may come into play. Teachers who are knowingly sexist will not want to display their usual unfair treatment towards female students as they will be concerned that this will get back to their head teacher. There are several practical issues that can be discussed in researching teachers such as timetable constraints and teachers being 'overworked and busy people'. These factors may make it difficult for a researcher to arrange an interview or get a good response rate from a questionnaire. In terms of observations, teachers may be reluctant to allow the researcher access to 'their classroom' and have the additional task of providing the researcher with a lesson plan.

Parents

It is possible that parents may see the researcher as just another teacher or even 'social worker in disguise', again leading to theoretical issues. Their responses to questionnaires and interviews may lack validity due to them not wanting to be seen as a 'bad parent'. The biggest practical problem with researching parents is access, as they are not usually in school! A good research opportunity for sociologists is a parents' evening. However, as middle-class parents are more likely to attend, the sample may not be representative. Even if they attend, working-class parents who possess 'anti-school' attitudes may be reluctant to participate in an interview or open up if they see the researcher as middle class. In addition, parents from ethnic minority backgrounds may have language barriers which may affect the validity of responses.

Exam tip

You should relate theoretical issues to practical concerns. For example, state that if students are rushing to complete a self-complete questionnaire or interview as the bell for lunch has just gone, their responses are likely to lack validity.

Exam tip

Be prepared to relate points specifically to the method. For questionnaires, for example, refer to pupils 'ticking any box' while for interviews you could refer to teachers not wanting to 'respond' to certain questions when asked.

Exam tip

Be prepared to discuss and evaluate strategies that a sociologist might employ to encourage a higher response rate, such as keeping the interviews or questionnaire short or paying for a supply teacher so that a teacher does not have to give up their own time for an interview. You should also evaluate such strategies in terms of whether they may reduce the validity of data or add to the cost of the research.

Exam tip

Remember to discuss strategies a sociologist might adopt to overcome the problem of access to parents, such as sending self-complete questionnaires via pupils, and to apply these to the context of studying education, e.g. the school's permission will still need to be obtained, certain parents are more likely to return the questionnaire and some pupils will not even take them home.

Schools

One of the main problems facing a sociologist when studying schools is the practical issue of access. Consent needs to be obtained from gatekeepers such as the head teacher or school governors for the research to go ahead. Even if this is achieved, head teachers may deny access to certain areas of the school or certain times of the year such as during exams. Researchers may not be allowed to observe teachers perceived by head teachers as 'poor' as they may be concerned that this may reflect badly on the image of the school. However, once access is gained, sociologists have the major practical strength of having a captive audience and having a ready-made sample stratified by year groups. Pupils are used to filling out questionnaires and as they feel they will get in trouble if they do not complete them, a high response rate can be obtained. Group interviews can be arranged relatively easily but schools are busy places and there may be problems with finding classrooms to use for interviews. In terms of documents and official statistics, there is a wide range of information available. Schools have to provide certain information by law, such as on attendance, and statistics such as exam results and documents like Ofsted reports are in the public domain and easily available via the internet. However, schools have a duty of care towards their pupils and access to documentation such as school reports may be denied. Theoretical problems of lack of validity can be applied to education statistics, such as schools manipulating truancy rates in order to boost their position in the 'education market'.

If the question is on a secondary method rather than a primary one, do not panic! You can use some of the points that refer to primary methods and discuss how official statistics and documents *do not* have these problems. For example, sociologists using official statistics do not have go through the problems of access and gatekeepers, as they are secondary data and in the public domain.

Level 3 (L3) — application

In order to achieve an A-grade response, the strengths and weaknesses of the method must be applied to the topic raised in the question and the item. For example, if the question is on using unstructured interviews to study the topic of material deprivation and achievement, the following would be an example of a L3 response:

> **Parents may give socially desirable responses which lack validity in the interview as they want to be seen as a supportive parent. For example, working-class parents may not want to discuss with a researcher that they don't buy their son or daughter a sociology revision guide because they cannot afford to as they are on the minimum wage.**

Exam tip

Remember to relate practical strengths such as having a 'captive audience' to theoretical strengths such as this leading to a potentially representative sample.

Exam tip

Try to develop the issue of access into schools to other practical issues such as the need for a CRB check which adds time and cost to the research.

Exam tip

Be prepared to apply contemporary issues to potential problems of using different methods. For example, despite exam results being generally regarded as 'hard' official statistics, schools have been found guilty of malpractice in relation to exam entries and manipulating data in order to improve their position in league tables.

It is much better to have two or three L3 points developed than list six or seven. You only need to use L3s well *twice* to get maximum marks. Two good L3 points are enough as long as you have three or four good L2s and a sound knowledge of the method in question.

Remember that you do not need to mention studies for the Methods in context question. If you do use them, it should be to illustrate a strength or weakness of the method in relation to the context of studying education or the topic.

Note that if the question refers to a specific group such as parents you can still refer to other groups that sociologists may wish to study. For example, if the question refers to student subcultures, you should still discuss that researchers may wish to obtain the views of teachers and parents on this topic.

Examinable skills

AQA Sociology examination papers are designed to test certain defined skills. These skills are expressed as assessment objectives (AOs) and are the same for AS and A-level, though the weighting given to each differs between the two levels. There are three AOs and it is important that you know what these are and what you have to be able to do in an exam to show your ability in each. Further guidance on each of the AOs is given in the guidance and comments. In practice, many answers to questions, particularly those carrying the higher marks, will contain elements of all three AOs.

Assessment objective 1 (AO1)

Demonstrate knowledge and understanding of:
- **sociological theories, concepts and evidence**
- **sociological research methods**

Your exam answers will have to demonstrate clearly to the examiners that your knowledge is accurate and appropriate to the topic being discussed and that you have a clear understanding of it. It is not enough simply to reproduce knowledge learned by rote. You must be able to use this knowledge in a meaningful way to answer the specific question set. This means that you must be able to *select* the appropriate knowledge from everything you know and use only the knowledge that is relevant to, and addresses the issues raised by, the question.

Assessment objective 2 (AO2)

Apply sociological theories, concepts, evidence and research methods to a range of issues.

In certain questions in the exam you will be presented with an item — a short paragraph setting the context for the question that is to follow, and providing you with some information to help answer it. You *must* take this relevant information and use (apply) it in your answer. However, 'applying' the material does not mean simply copying it from the item and leaving it to speak for itself. You will need to show your understanding of the material by doing something with it, such as offering a criticism, explaining something about it, linking it to a particular sociological theory or offering another example of what is being stated or suggested. You will therefore be using your own knowledge to add to the information that you have been given and will be *applying* it appropriately to answer the question.

Assessment objective 3 (AO3)

Analyse and evaluate sociological theories, concepts, evidence and research methods in order to:

- **present arguments**
- **make judgements**
- **draw conclusions**

The skill of *analysis* is shown by breaking something down into its component parts and subjecting them to detailed examination. Analysis is shown by providing answers (depending, of course, on what it is that you are analysing) to questions such as 'who said or who believes this?', 'what does this concept relate to?', 'what does this research method entail?', 'how was this evidence collected?' and so on. The skill of *evaluation* is shown by the ability to identify the strengths and weaknesses or limitations of any sociological material. It is not sufficient, however, simply to list the strengths or limitations of something — you need to be able to say *why* something is considered a strength or otherwise, and sometimes you will need to state *who* claims that this is a strength or weakness. Depending on what it is you are discussing, you may be able to reach a conclusion about the relative merits or otherwise of something, but remember that any conclusions should be based on the rational arguments and solid sociological evidence that you have presented in your answer.

Weighting of assessment objectives

In the exam papers, each AO is given a particular weighting, which indicates its relative importance to the overall mark gained. The weightings are not the same for AS and A-level, so be sure that you look at the one that is appropriate for the exam you will be taking.

Assessment objective	Paper 1 (approximate %)	Paper 2 (approximate %)	Overall weighting
AO1	22	24	46
AO2	18	13	31
AO3	10	13	23
Overall	50	50	100

Table 12 Weighting for AS examinations

Assessment objective	Paper 1 (approximate %)	Paper 2 (approximate %)	Paper 3 (approximate %)	Overall weighting
AO1	15	13	16	44
AO2	11	11	9	31
AO3	8	9	8	25
Overall	33.33	33.33	33.33	100

Table 13 Weighting for A-level examinations

Command words

Ofqual, the body that sets the criteria for all GCE sociology specifications, has an approved list of 'command words' that are used in exam questions. The following are some of the most commonly used, but it is important to remember that the list is not exhaustive, and that occasionally other, similar, words or phrases may be used instead. This shows how important it is to take time in an exam and read the questions very carefully before you start writing. It is worth learning what is meant by these command words, to ensure that you give an appropriate response.

Define Give the meaning of something

Explain Give purposes or reasons

Outline Give the main characteristics

Outline and explain Give the main characteristics and develop these

Using one example, briefly explain Use an example to give a brief account of something

Analyse Separate information into components and identify their characteristics

Evaluate Make judgements from the available evidence

Applying material from the item Draw on the material provided and develop it using your own knowledge to answer the question. (Remember to make use of the item, but not to copy from it — see page 44.)

■ Test paper 1

AS Paper 1: Education with methods in context

(01) Define the term 'marketisation' of education.   (2 marks)

ⓔ It is useful to give an example to illustrate how education is run like a business.

(02) Using one example, briefly explain how material deprivation may affect educational achievement.   (2 marks)

ⓔ You must apply your explanation clearly to achievement to score full marks. Be careful to refer to material rather than cultural factors.

(03) Outline three ways in which Marxists see school as being similar to the workplace.   (6 marks)

ⓔ Concepts such as hierarchy and alienation will need to be explained for full marks.

(04) Outline and explain two reasons why different pupil subcultures exist in schools.   (10 marks)

ⓔ Remember that there is no point in listing a range of reasons for subcultures that you may be aware of. Pick the two that you feel you are best able to explain in approximately 15 minutes.

(05) Read Item A below and answer the question that follows.

Item A

The education system is one of the most important institutions in society. Marxists have a very negative view of its role in capitalist society, arguing that it serves the interests of the ruling class in a variety of ways.

For example, Althusser argues that the education system is an ideological state apparatus which helps to reproduce and legitimise existing class inequalities. While some sociologists claim that the education system is based on equal opportunities, Marxists would argue that the idea that education is a meritocracy is a myth.

Applying material from Item A and your knowledge, evaluate the contribution that Marxism has made to our understanding of the role of education.   (20 marks)

ⓔ Use Template 2 (on page 47) for an item-based essay question. Make sure that as well as evaluation from other theories such as functionalism, postmodernism and the New Right, you include specific evaluation of the Marxist view on the role of education. Remember that evaluation includes both positive and negative points.

(06) Read Item B below and answer the question that follows.

Item B

Investigating the role of parents in pupils' achievement

Evidence suggests that there is a close correlation between parental involvement and pupils' achievement. Sociologists have identified a range of cultural and material factors such as attitudes to school and differences in parents' income levels. In relation to class and ethnic differences, the language spoken in the home and access to educational resources may affect pupils' achievement.

Structured interviews can be carried out relatively easily using a large number of students and teachers. The findings can also be used in order to establish patterns and trends in achievement in relation to factors such as how much support parents give. However, there may be practical problems in gaining access and some parents may feel that questions are too personal and that they are being judged.

> **Applying material from Item B and your knowledge of research methods, evaluate the strengths and limitations of using structured interviews to investigate the role of parents in pupils' achievement.** (20 marks)

e Make sure you use the general L2 points outlined on pages 48–50. The second paragraph of the item gives you some strengths and limitations of structured interviews, so make sure you use them as well as others you may know. Try to apply these clearly to study the topic of the role of parents in pupils' achievement. You will get some ideas on how to do this from the first paragraph but remember not to just copy from the item. You could structure your answer around PET (see page 45) but make sure that you apply the method to L2 and L3 issues in each paragraph.

Student A

01 This is when education is run more like a business. Parents are the customers which schools have to compete for by offering a better 'service' than their rivals (other schools).

---

e **2/2 marks awarded.** An appropriate definition and example are given.

---
02 Poor housing can lead to overcrowding. This may mean there is not a good environment to study or do homework which may mean that school work will suffer.

---

e **2/2 marks awarded.** An appropriate example is explained and linked to achievement.

03 ■ Alienation. Just like workers students have a lack of control over what times they have to eat and work.

■ Hierarchy. Both students and workers have to accept authority from people above them (teachers and bosses).

■ Competition. Just as students are encouraged to work hard to be 'top of the class' workers are encouraged to compete with each other for promotion.

ⓔ 6/6 marks awarded. Three appropriate examples explained.

04 An internal reason why subcultures may exist in schools is in response to teacher labelling. Interactionists such as Becker argued that as a result of working-class pupils being labelled as 'deviant' by teachers they may feel that there is little point in trying to work in school and so they underachieve. As a result they may join a peer group of other working-class students who have been similarly labelled. Once part of this peer group, students may develop anti-school values and gain status in ways other than working hard such as truanting. As well as individual teachers, schools may create subcultures by streaming. By placing students (usually working class) into bottom streams they are even more likely to develop an anti-school culture as they have been further labelled as 'failures' who are only capable of doing bottom-set work. On the other hand students in the top stream (usually middle class) are likely to develop a pro-school subculture. As a result they will be committed to the values of the school and gain status through their academic success. Lacey referred to these two opposite ways of responding to streaming as polarisation. Labelling and streaming can work together to lead to a self-fulfilling prophecy of failure. As working-class pupils are negatively labelled they would be more likely to be placed in a lower stream which they would see as being for 'no hopers'. Collectively the bottom set would give up on school and gain status in their group by misbehaving and forming a delinquent subculture.

However, there are criticisms of the view that labelling and streaming will lead to subcultures forming in this simplistic way. As Fuller showed, pupils are not passive and can reject teacher labels. However, the black girls in her study still ended up forming an anti-school subculture due to what they saw as the racist labelling of the teachers but it was pro-education as they worked hard to achieve. It could also be argued that it is unlikely that subcultures will develop in this way today as students are rarely streamed in schools and have the opportunity to move up and down sets. Students are less likely to join an anti-school subculture if they are in different sets for different subjects. Subcultures may also be caused by external factors such as the working-class values. Willis' lads had a working-class counter-school culture which challenged the school which they saw as a waste of time. Rather than their subculture being caused by the internal factor of teacher labelling, the anti-school subculture of the lads resulted from the working-class values from their home background.

ⓔ **10/10 marks awarded.** The internal reasons of teacher labelling and streaming are well explained and applied to the formation of subcultures. The account has a range of concepts and is located within a theoretical framework. There are also two good evaluation points on labelling and streaming. The last point on Willis could be seen as a third reason for why subcultures exist, which is not required as the question only asks for two. However, the point scores as it is used as an evaluation of internal factors causing the formation of subcultures.

> **05** As Item A states, Marxists such as Althusser have a critical view of the role of education and believe that it plays an important role for capitalism in controlling people's ideas and maintaining inequality. However, functionalists reject the Marxist approach and argue that education has a number of positive functions such as secondary socialisation.

ⓔ A good start following AAA as outlined in Template 2 and material from Item A is used well.

> Althusser believes that the education system reproduces inequality as the working class continually have a negative experience in school, making them fail through the generations. Therefore working-class pupils will never hold a positive view of education due to the negative experience of their parents who believe education is worthless. As a result they will fail in education and so they will end up with the same jobs as their parents. Furthermore, Althusser believes that the legitimisation of inequality in education is produced through ideologies. He believes that the education system tries to convince pupils that inequality is inevitable and is down to the individual's fault and not down to the capitalist system. The legitimisation of inequality affects the way these pupils view themselves in that they accept their lower position in capitalist society and do not challenge it. Althusser argues that in this way education acts as an ideological state apparatus (ISA). However, critics would argue that this is a simplistic view and that the education system is not just used to control ideas.

ⓔ This is an accurate account of Althusser, if a little descriptive. A good specific evaluation point is made at the end regarding education being an ISA although this could have been developed.

> Secondly, Marxists Bowles and Gintis also believe that education legitimates inequality due to the 'myth of meritocracy'. They argue against the functionalists' view of meritocracy and argue that achievement is based on family background rather than effort and ability. Bowles and Gintis argue that the myth of meritocracy disguises the fact that higher-class pupils succeed because of their class rather than through equal opportunities and hard work. This therefore helps legitimate inequality and means that it will be less likely for the working class to overthrow capitalism as they are more likely to accept inequality as inevitable and 'fair'.

Questions & Answers

(e) A good comparison with functionalism is made on the issue of meritocracy but some evaluation of the Marxist view would have been useful.

> Furthermore, Bowles and Gintis put forward the idea of 'the correspondence principle'. This is the idea that the education system mirrors the ways of work. To support their view they suggested that schools teach pupils to accept a hierarchy. Schools do this by having a head teacher as the 'boss' and pupils as the 'workers'. The hidden curriculum is also used to make students accept authority such as wearing uniform. Schools also mirror competition as the way in which pupils are put into sets and are expected to obtain higher grades mirrors the way a workplace has differences in status and pay. Lastly, alienation in schools, where pupils have no choice over what work they do and when they do it, mirrors the way in which workers are expected to do certain jobs when and how they want you to do it.

(e) Some good use of concepts and some points have been developed well with examples. While there is an example of the hidden curriculum, its connection to the correspondence principle could have been more clearly explained. There is no specific evaluation.

> Bowles and Gintis argue that working-class pupils are taught to accept inequality by the education system. However, Willis' study on the 12 'lads' suggests that working-class pupils can see through the ideology of education and its attempts to indoctrinate. Willis' study showed that working-class males truanted and resisted the school's rules because they thought they were superior to conformist students (the 'ear'oles') and that the school was a waste of time. 'The lads' wanted to do manual work to show off their masculinity and therefore they failed at school. As a result class inequality was reproduced because their counter-school culture meant they would end up in working-class jobs.

(e) A good evaluation point made with Willis; however, this could have been identified as a neo-Marxist view.

> In conclusion, perhaps the main strength of the Marxist view on the role of education is its emphasis on class inequality. Marxists demonstrate how the education system reproduces and legitimates inequality through various points such as the myth of meritocracy. A main strength of Bowles and Gintis' view on the myth of meritocracy is that statistics on how the working class achieve show that they are much less likely to go on to higher education than the middle class. However, many disagree with this view as postmodernists would argue that the education system no longer produces inequality but rather produces diversity. Functionalists totally reject the Marxist view and argue that education performs vital socialising functions such as ensuring that there are shared values in society. Another weakness argued by feminists is that Willis' study ignores gender as it was only about 'the lads' from one school. This study was therefore not representative and we cannot generalise the findings. Other sociologists argue that Marxists

only focus on class and that as well as gender they fail to acknowledge other inequalities such as ethnicity.

e Some good evaluation in the conclusion. However, some of these points could have been included earlier in the essay (such as the criticism of Willis) and some need more explanation. For example, the point on postmodernism could have been related to a criticism of the correspondence principle and that more diversity in the economy today requires the education system to produce a more diverse workforce.

e **18/20 marks awarded.** Overall this essay displays a range of accurate and detailed knowledge on three key Marxist views of the role of education. There is some good analysis but evaluation would have been more effective if it had been introduced throughout the essay. For example, functionalist views on the positive nature of the socialisation function could have been used as a critique of Bowles and Gintis.

06 Structured interviews (SI) are when a list of pre-prepared questions, usually closed, are read out to the respondent by a trained interviewer. Positivists would prefer to use SIs as they are reliable due to using standardised questions. They would argue that the quantitative data gained from the pre-coded questions could be used to test a hypothesis such as whether material deprivation causes working-class underachievement. Interpretivists, however, would argue that SI lacked validity. In the case of investigating the role of parents they would argue that unstructured interviews would be a much better method to use to gain verstehen on parents', teachers' and pupils' opinions on how this can influence underachievement.

e This introduction follows WWWE as outlined in Template 1 well and shows good understanding of the method. There is a brief attempt at application towards the end but this is not developed. It is a good idea to abbreviate words that will frequently be used in the answer as this will save time.

As the item states, a major problem of researching in schools is access as permission needs to be obtained from head teachers and parents. For example, in order to interview pupils a researcher will need a CRB check which adds to practical issues of cost and time. One of the main practical strengths of SI is that it is quick and fairly cheap to administer and it is also time efficient due to the pre-coded nature of the questions. All this may mean that a head teacher is more likely to allow access if the research can be conducted quickly so disruption to lessons is kept to a minimum. However, a school may be unwilling to let researchers discuss sensitive issues with pupils or teachers. For example, they might not want them being questioned about how well the school communicates and involves parents. A head teacher would not want the school to be seen in a bad light as this would have a negative effect on the position in the league tables.

Questions & Answers

ⓔ Some good L2 application on access issues in studying schools, using the item as a trigger. Some points are developed with practical issues related to the method. There is an attempt at L3 application in the penultimate sentence. This contains a good specific reference to the method with the use of the word 'questioned'.

> As they are not in school parents would be more difficult to access. However, they may be more willing to take part in a SI at a parents' evening if the researcher can guarantee that it will only take a few minutes. This relates to another advantage of SI that it may have a higher response rate than questionnaires sent through the post as it is more difficult to refuse as it's face to face. A parent may be more willing to take part in an interview at a parents' evening as they may want to give the impression that they are concerned about their child's education. The issue that parents would not want to be seen as a 'bad parent' in a SI could however lead to a theoretical problem of lack of validity in terms of the support they give. Parents might not want to admit that they are not very involved in helping their child or that they don't have time to support them. As a result socially desirable answers may be given such as saying that they spend two hours a night helping with homework when in fact they have to work a night shift in their factory job.

ⓔ Again some good L2 application developed, this time in relation to studying parents, with a good example of a research opportunity. There is some good L3 application at the end with the example of parents' responses on homework, which is well tied in with theoretical issues.

> Interpretivists would also argue that SI lack validity due to their inflexible nature and the imposition problem. The researcher has decided what is important in terms of the parents' role in achievement in advance and this may not coincide with what the interviewee may think. For example, the set questions asked may not reflect the parents' experiences of supporting their child with school work but it is impossible for them to raise an issue such as the importance of their local Sure Start centre in developing their parenting skills. Similarly, a teacher will know more than the researcher about internal factors in school such as student subcultures that influence a pupil's achievement. Students may also see researchers as 'teachers in disguise' so may not be willing to give valid answers in structured interviews. The language used in the questions in the SI would need to be simple as students may struggle to understand sociological concepts.

ⓔ Some very sophisticated L3 application here with the characteristic of the method, the imposition problem, being applied to a factor relating to parental support. Some good L2 examples of application but these are listed and have not been applied to the topic.

> There are relatively few ethical issues with SI as the participant can control whether they want to answer. However, the researcher still needs to ensure anonymity and obtain informed consent. As well as obtaining consent from parents the researcher will have to consider whether the students are mature enough to understand what the research is about. It may be that discussing sensitive issues such as how much support they get from their parents may cause students harm. If the question in the SI is about how often their parents go to parents' evenings they might be too embarrassed and upset to tell a researcher that the answer is never.

ⓔ Good examples of ethical issues applied to the method and studying children. There is some L3 application at the end in relation to potential harm and parental involvement.

ⓔ **20/20 marks awarded.** This essay demonstrates a sound knowledge of the method. It is conceptually detailed and has a range of PET and L2 application, some of which is developed. This would score 16/20 on its own. However, the three developed examples of L3 application means this response scores full marks. While a conclusion is a key component of an education or methods essay, it is not necessary for an A-grade answer in the Methods in context question.

ⓔ **Total score: 58/60 marks = a top grade A**

Student B

01 This is supply and demand which involves meeting the needs of consumers.

ⓔ 1/2 marks awarded. This has a notion of marketisation but is not applied to education.

02 Lack of diet. Working class do not ensure that they give their children the 5 a day that they need.

ⓔ 1/2 marks awarded. An example of material deprivation is identified but the explanation refers to a cultural issue and is not applied to achievement.

03 Hierarchy, fragmentation and the hidden curriculum.

ⓔ 2/6 marks awarded. The first two responses are both partial as they are examples of the correspondence principle but are not explained. The third response does not score as it only applies to education.

> **04** Different subcultures may exist in schools due to a lack of interest in a subject. If pupils don't achieve very highly they may give up. One reason why subcultures may exist in schools is due to teacher labelling. If a pupil isn't very clever and a teacher labels them as thick they may not try hard to achieve and may rebel. This may lead to the self-fulfilling prophecy when they realise that the teacher had labelled them they react by not trying. Pupil subcultures may have something to do with what teachers expect from them. Becker found that the way a teacher acts towards a student depends on how close they fit to the 'ideal student'. If the student doesn't fit this then the teacher might treat them differently, e.g. give them less attention. This may lead to a group of students feeling that they don't live up to this label so they get together to form a subculture within the school.

ⓔ **4/10 marks awarded.** This response falls into the middle band (4–7 marks) as it identifies a cause of subcultures, teacher labelling, and has some brief analysis and use of concepts. However, the account only just demonstrates reasonable knowledge and is only applied to the formation of subcultures towards the end of the response.

> **05** Althusser argues that education is 'an ideological state apparatus which helps to reproduce and legitimise existing class inequalities' as stated in Item A. Marxists such as Althusser argue that education is an ideological state apparatus. They believe that the role of education is reproducing class inequalities. However, functionalists reject this view as they see the role of education positively as it gives equal opportunities.

ⓔ An attempt at using AAA as outlined in Template 2; however, material from the item should be 'used' rather than quoted.

> Althusser argues that education is an important ideological state apparatus (ISA) that helps to control people's ideas and beliefs. He believes that education has two purposes: it reproduces class inequalities by ensuring that most working-class pupils experience educational failure, and it legitimates this inequality, by persuading the working class to accept this failure as their fault. As a result the education system controls the working class and makes them accept inequality. In this way Althusser argues that they are less likely to rebel against capitalism.

ⓔ The candidate develops the item and gives a brief analysis of Althusser, but this paragraph lacks any evaluation.

> Bowles and Gintis argue that capitalism requires a workforce with the kind of attitudes, behaviour and personality-type suited to their role as alienated and exploited workers. They need to be willing to accept hard work, low pay and orders from their bosses. They found from their study that students who showed independence and creativity (those who might question authority)

tended to gain low grades. However, those who were obedient and disciplined were more likely to gain high grades. Bowles and Gintis describe the education system as 'a giant myth-making machine'. They argue that meritocracy does not in fact exist and that school mirrors the workplace. Bowles and Gintis conclude from their evidence that schooling helps to produce the obedient workers that capitalism needs. They do not believe that education fosters personal development; rather that it stunts and distorts students' development.

e A fair account of Bowles and Gintis but this could have been developed with use of the correspondence principle and the hidden curriculum. The link between social class and the myth of meritocracy also needs to be made more clearly. The attempt at evaluation at the end should have been linked to the functionalist view.

Neo-Marxist Willis investigated the way schooling serves capitalism. Willis used an interpretivist approach and carried out unstructured group interviews to uncover the meanings of the counter-school culture of the 'lads'. These interviews allowed the lads to talk freely in their own words about the way they viewed school, teachers and work. He found that the lads had an anti-school culture that was like the culture of their dads who worked in factories. Just like their dads, they saw manual work as superior to intellectual work which they saw as feminine. Willis agrees with Bowles and Gintis that the working class fail. However, he rejects Bowles and Gintis' ideas as students can reject the school values and the hidden curriculum.

e A good attempt to outline how Willis used an interpretivist approach and the study is used to evaluate Bowles and Gintis. However, the account fails to clearly explain why the lads failed and ended up in working-class jobs.

Functionalists have a different view on the role of education. Postmodernists take a diversity approach. They argue class is no longer important as society has become more diverse and fragmented and the economy has become post-Fordist.

e Two alternative views are presented but they are not applied as a criticism of the Marxist view on the role of education.

The main strength of the Marxist view on the role of education is its emphasis on its class conflict approach and that class inequalities exist. However, as functionalists argue, Marxists fail to acknowledge that school reproduces not only capitalism, but patriarchy too.

e An attempt at a conclusion but the point on Marxism is quite general and the candidate has incorrectly linked functionalism to a feminist criticism.

ⓔ **13/20 marks awarded.** Overall three key Marxist views of the role of education have been identified but with only limited analysis. There are some attempts to evaluate in most paragraphs but these again lack any real depth and are merely stated, or lack application to the question. A good evaluation point that both candidates could have made is that the Marxist view of the role of education is that it is out of date. For example, postmodernists would argue that Willis' emphasis on the importance of manual work is no longer applicable in a post-Fordist economy.

> **06** One of the main strengths for using structured interviews within schools is that it is easy to quantify the results, so they are easy to understand and compare. Quantitative data is data that can be counted, as in the word quantity, and is used in questionnaires, and structured interviews. However, structured interviews can be also qualitative, as the question could be open or closed. Closed questions have restricted yes/no categories, so you cannot elaborate your answers, while open questions can have long answers, with a lot of detail, and a more truthful view. Structured interviews tend to be a favoured method of positivists. Positivists believe that sociology can be studied as a science, with quantitative data.

ⓔ A reasonable start in terms of knowledge on the method but the candidate has not followed the WWWE outlined in Template 1. No application of the method to studying education or the topic of role of parents.

> One of the main strengths is the high response rates; this is shown through the study by Young and Willmott (1962), who used structured interviews to research into the extended family in east London. Out of 987 people approached only 54 refused. This shows that it is harder to turn down a face-to-face interviewer than, for example, a questionnaire through the post. Although this was a success in 1962, in today's society there is a greater reluctance to take part in a structured interview in the street as people are too busy.

ⓔ The candidate makes a good point about structured interviews and response rates but this is not applied to the question. Listing the 'detail' on studies is generally not a good strategy and is not required for the Methods in context question. This study does not even relate to education.

> When investigating the role of parents in pupils' achievement, structured interviews are easy and quick to carry out and are therefore also cheap. Other methods, such as unstructured interviews, can take a lot longer to do and you may only get a small group that is very unrepresentative of the topic. Questions within the structured interviews could include questions on home language and access to educational resources.

🄮 A good attempt at comparative analysis via the use of unstructured interviews; however, there is still no application. The last sentence at first appears to be an attempt at application but is just copied from the item so does not score.

> However, with structured interviews, closed questions might not present a true image of the parents' involvement. Parents might be asked questions that they feel are too personal, that they are being judged, and may give false data. Also, there may not be enough information within closed questions to get a true representation of a parent's involvement. This is a theoretical criticism that interpretivists would make of structured interviews that the data gained lacks validity.

🄮 Again, the second sentence is just copied from the item! A strength, however, is that the student has categorised the problem of lack of validity as theoretical and located it within a methodological perspective by referring to interpretivism.

> As the item suggests a major problem will be access. Permission from gatekeepers such as the head teacher (to gain access to the school) and parents (to gain consent to speak to their children) would be required. Teachers usually are very busy during the school day and researchers would need to work around the teacher's timetable. Parents are also likely to give socially desirable answers so their responses will not be valid.

🄮 The student has some good examples of application to the research characteristics of studying schools via reference to gatekeepers and timetable constraints. However, these are listed rather than being developed and are not linked into the topic of the role of parents. The last sentence does not score in terms of application as socially desirable answers could be given by any group of respondents. In order to gain marks for L3 application the candidate would need to specifically explain why parents might give such answers in relation to their role in their child's achievement (see Student A's answer).

> In conclusion, structured interviews can be useful in investigating the role of parents in pupils' achievements due to the quantitative data that they gain. However, as interpretivists argue, this data lacks validity.

🄮 While there is an attempt at a conclusion it is simply a recap of points already made and therefore adds nothing to the response.

🄮 13/20 marks awarded. Overall the student has outlined some reasonable knowledge on the method and has some brief analysis and good use of theory. There are some stated examples of L2 application on the context of studying education. However, there is no L3 application on the topic of investigating the role of parents in pupils' achievements.

🄮 Total score: 34/60 marks = a low grade C

■ Test paper 2

AS Paper 2 (Section A): Research methods

(01) Outline two problems of using laboratory experiments in sociological research. **(4 marks)**

ⓔ Make sure you refer to specific problems of laboratory experiments and not field experiments.

(02) Evaluate the problems of using overt participant observation in sociological research. **(16 marks)**

ⓔ Use Template 1 for methods questions on page 45. Make sure you focus on overt PO and only use other types of observation for comparative analysis and evaluation.

> **Student A**
>
> **01** ■ Hawthorne effect, as if people know they are being observed their behaviour may change.
>
> ■ They lack ecological validity as they take place in an artificial environment.
>
> ■ They may cause both physical and mental harm to the participants.

ⓔ 4/4 marks awarded. All three responses are correct. It is a good strategy to use bullet points and give an extra example just in case one of the first two is incorrect.

> **02** Overt participant observation (OPO) is a form of observation in which the researcher makes their true identity and purpose known. OPO is favoured by interpretivists as it provides a valid, first-hand insight as the researcher is actually joining in with the activities of those being studied. However, positivists reject the use of OPO due to its lack of reliability, generalisability and representativeness. Positivists would prefer to use overt non-participant observation as this would more easily allow the researcher to use a structured observation schedule which could be used to gain reliable data due to its standardised nature.

ⓔ Good use of WWWE as outlined in Template 1 and good comparison with non-participant observation.

> One of the practical issues of OPO is 'getting in'. Groups such as criminal gangs would be unlikely to allow a researcher access to study them as they may see them as the 'police in disguise'. An example of this is Patrick, who

> could only gain access to the 'Glasgow gang' through a gang leader. He was not able to reveal his true identity to the other gang members and so had to conduct covert participant observation (CPO). With OPO the group being studied may prevent the researcher from seeing certain things as happened in Punch's study where the two Amsterdam police officers told him afterwards that they only let him see what they wanted. This leads to a theoretical problem of lack of validity as Punch may not have seen their usual behaviour such as racist treatment of ethnic minorities when they were on patrol.

ⓔ Practical problems of access are well explained via comparison with CPO. A good link to a theoretical problem is made with an appropriate example. There are, however, no attempts to evaluate in terms of the strengths of the method.

> 'Staying in' can raise practical issues in terms of fitting in with the group. This is not such a problem with OPO compared to CPO as the researcher does not need to convince the group he or she is 'one of them'. However, again it could lead to a lack of valid data as if the group do not trust the researcher they are unlikely to be given full access to the group's activities. However, a practical advantage in Barker's OPO study is that, unlike CPO, she could take notes openly. However, this study illustrates another practical problem of OPO which is that it is often time-consuming and expensive compared to a more structured and controlled method such as non- participant observation or questionnaires.

ⓔ Practical problems are again well explained and evaluation of the method is developed by comparison of a strength as well as weakness of the method as compared to CPO.

> Positivists have a number of theoretical issues with OPO. OPO studies such as Punch's on two police officers due to its small sample size would be seen an unrepresentative. They would argue that unlike questionnaires that can have a large sample the results from OPO cannot be generalised. Observation is also difficult to replicate due to the unique circumstances of the situation and the group being observed and so lacks reliability. An additional theoretical problem with OPO is the risk of the Hawthorne effect, in which the people being observed change their normal behaviour patterns because they know they are being observed. People may adopt the 'halo effect' in order to appear better than they really are, meaning the results are invalid. The most well-known example of this is at the Hawthorne plant where employees worked harder simply because they were being watched and not because the conditions in which they were working changed.

ⓔ This is a very good paragraph, which differentiates between different types of theoretical problems.

A major strength of OPO that interpretivists would point to is that it provides a valuable insight to the group's behaviour. It allows the researcher to see what people do rather that what they say they do, as happens in methods such as questionnaires. As Barker's study illustrates, a potential strength of OPO is that the researcher could become seen as a 'trusted outsider'. As Barker spent over 6 years with the Moonies she developed a rapport and may have gained valid data as a result. As Barker was overt she was also able to use interviews and questionnaires to check the validity of her observations. However, a problem with 'staying in' with overt observation is 'going native'. Barker became very close to some of the 'Moonies' as she studied them for so long and this may have affected the validity of her findings.

(e) This paragraph drifts into a discussion of strengths but does tie these in with problems in the final two sentences.

As OPO is an 'honest' method it does not have many ethical issues. Unlike CPO you are not lying to or deceiving anyone. However, you may have to guarantee anonymity to those involved as they could be put in danger or get into trouble if their identity is revealed. Researchers may also end up witnessing illegal or immoral activity during OPO and as a result the researcher would have the ethical dilemma of whether to inform the police. 'Getting out' can raise ethical issues as the researcher may find it hard to leave a group they have become attached to. This would not be an issue with non-participant observation as the sociologist does not take part in the activities of the group and so is less likely to develop a rapport with those studied.

(e) This is a good evaluative paragraph, which compares ethical strengths and weaknesses of the method.

Perhaps the biggest problem with overt participant observation is the theoretical issue of the data lacking validity due to the Hawthorne effect as participants 'put on a show' for the researcher. A possible solution to this is for the researcher to be 'semi-overt', meaning some information is shared and some hidden. For example, Whyte only revealed his identity to a key member of a gang and told the rest he was writing a book about their neighbourhood rather than studying them. The usefulness of OPO also depends on what is being studied as clearly it is not suitable for topics such as domestic violence. While interpretivists would argue OPO can lead to valid data, it does not provide the insight that CPO can obtain due to it being an 'honest' method.

(e) The candidate identifies a key problem and solution with application of a study. Something 'new' is introduced and another good comparison with CPO is made.

e 16/16 marks awarded. This is a well-structured essay following Template 1. Problems are categorised well in terms of PET and a range of studies are well applied to problems of OPO. The strengths of the method are generally well tied in to problems of OPO and there are several attempts at comparative analysis with other types of observation and more structured methods.

Total score: 20/20 marks = a top grade A

01 ■ Ethical issues.
■ It is difficult to isolate a single variable that can influence social behaviour, which is often complex. This is shown in Bandura's experiment about violence and the media. The children were meant to behave more violently after being exposed to violence. There may have been other extraneous variables that may have caused them to be more violent that the researcher was not aware of.

e 2/4 marks awarded. The first point does not score as ethical issues needs to be qualified (as is done in the third point of Candidate A's answer). While the second point scores, the candidate has wasted valuable time by giving unnecessary detail of the Bandura study. The first sentence was enough for 2 marks.

02 Overt observation is a form of observation where the researcher makes their identity and purpose known to those being studied. Covert observation is the opposite, when those being studied are deceived and no informed consent is gained. Observation can either be participant, where the researcher joins in, which is favoured by interpretivists, or non-participant, which positivists prefer.

e This is a 'catch all' introduction, defining different types of observation but not specifically addressing the method outlined in the question. It does not explain why interpretivists would prefer to use OPO or why positivists would not.

A big problem with overt participant observation is gaining access to the group you want to study. Some groups may not want to be studied, for example it was hard for Patrick to become a part of the Glasgow gang as they might not want people knowing about some of what they do. This is where covert observation is better as you don't tell the group you're studying them, so don't have to spend time convincing them to let you do so. Another problem with overt participant observation is that it could be time-consuming and the researcher could go native. For example, Maurice Punch began to act in a similar way to the police officers which he was observing, meaning he went native. This may have made it harder for him to adjust back to normal life and could also cause biased results.

ⓔ While there are a number of relevant points here, they are mostly listed and not explained (e.g. going native). Problems are not categorised as practical or theoretical and there is some confused knowledge on overt and covert with the use of Patrick's study. Patrick could have been used to discuss issues with OPO if the candidate had referred to the gang leader being informed about the purpose of the research (i.e. that it was 'semi-overt').

> There are a number of strengths of overt participant observation. As the participants know that they are being studied there are no ethical issues. You are not lying so there is no deception and the researcher doesn't have to take part in everything the group does such as illegal activities. The researcher can ask naive questions which they couldn't do with covert observation as it would blow their cover. As they have no cover to blow the researcher can take notes which will lead to more valid data than covert participant observation where they would have to rely on their memory and write up notes later. A final advantage is that they can also ask the groups if they can interview them or give them a questionnaire to fill in which again wouldn't be possible with covert participant observation.

ⓔ Some accurate strengths and good comparative analysis with CPO but there is no reference to the question, i.e. the problems of OPO.

> While there are few ethical issues with overt participant observation as there is informed consent, the researcher may have some moral dilemmas particularly if they are studying criminal groups. The researcher may witness illegal activities the gang is involved in, like Patrick being part of the extreme violence of the Glasgow gang. While there is no pressure on the researcher to commit a crime as they don't have to participate in all the activities, not reporting it to the police could be considered ethically wrong.

ⓔ This is the best paragraph in terms of AO2 and AO3 skills, despite the inaccurate use of Patrick.

> I think that the main problem with overt participant observation is the Hawthorne effect as if people know they are being observed they will behave in a socially desirable way. The main strength of overt participant observation is that there is no deception.

ⓔ This is a simplistically expressed conclusion and the strength is not linked to a problem.

ⓔ 11/16 marks awarded. While this candidate has identified a fair range of problems of OPO, there is limited analysis or evaluation. There is a reasonable discussion of ethical issues but strengths are for the most part not tied in to problems.

Total score: 13/20 marks = a high grade C

■Test paper 3

A-level Paper 1: Education with theory and methods

(01) Outline two cultural factors that may affect social class differences in educational achievement. **(4 marks)**

ⓔ Remember to make sure that they are 'cultural' factors, and that you focus on social class differences. It is useful to give an example to illustrate how each factor relates to achievement.

(02) Outline three ways in which government educational policies have attempted to reduce inequality in achievement between social classes. **(6 marks)**

ⓔ To gain full marks, you must show how each policy was intended to reduce inequality in achievement between social classes.

(03) Read Item A below and answer the question that follows.

> **Item A**
>
> Since the 1980s there has been a growing gender gap in achievement. In almost all subjects at GCSE level females have consistently outperformed males. The impact of feminism has widely been acknowledged as a key factor in the improved achievement of girls. However, despite gender differences in attitude and application, the educational performance of boys has also improved. While women are now more likely than men to go to university, a higher proportion of males get first-class degrees.

Applying material from Item A, analyse two reasons for gender differences in achievement. **(10 marks)**

ⓔ You are only required to give two reasons and these *must* be applied from material in the item. You could apply the 'impact of feminism' to both internal and external factors such as its impact on legislation and policies in school and wider society. Other triggers from the item that could be applied are the reference to different attitudes and application, GCSE exams, the difference in the award of first-class degrees and more women attending university. You should analyse your reasons in some depth but note that evaluation will also be rewarded. While this is a 'mini-essay' there is no need (or time!) to do an introduction, and a conclusion, if used at all, should be brief.

(04) Read Item B below and answer the question that follows.

> **Item B**
>
> According to figures from the DfE, pupils from Chinese and Indian backgrounds consistently perform better than white, Pakistani, Bangladeshi and black pupils at all stages of education. There are also important gender differences between ethnic groups in other areas within education. For example, permanent exclusion rates are usually highest for black Caribbean boys and lowest for Bangladeshi girls.
>
> Some sociologists argue that such differences can be explained by factors that occur in school such as teacher racism and bias in the school curriculum. However, other sociologists argue that factors outside school are more important.

Applying material from Item B and your own knowledge, evaluate the view that ethnic differences in educational achievement are primarily the result of factors inside school. (30 marks)

(e) As well as giving specific evaluation of internal factors, you should use external factors to evaluate the importance of factors inside school on ethnic differences in achievement. Refer to a variety of different ethnic groups, as stated in the item, and make sure that factors discussed are clearly linked to the achievement of these different groups. Also, make use of references in the item to gender and class affecting differences in ethnic achievement. Remember to use Template 2 for item-based essays outlined on page 47.

(05) Read Item C below and answer the question that follows.

Item C

Investigating the impact of pupils' subcultures on educational achievement

Some pupils in school belong to subcultures, meaning that they share a similar set of values and behaviour patterns. Through processes in schools such as labelling and streaming, pupils may be polarised into either pro- or anti-school subcultures. Sociologists have examined how these processes are often based on class, gender and ethnicity. For example, anti-school subcultures, where pupils in bottom sets may lack self-esteem and fail, are often dominated by working-class, male students from certain ethnic minority groups.

One way to investigate pupil subcultures is to use self-completion written questionnaires. These can allow respondents to answer anonymously on the reasons why pupils join subcultures. Students and teachers are used to filling in questionnaires in school and pupils could give them to their parents to complete at home. However, respondents may find questionnaires difficult to fill in on their own, particularly if the subject is on a complex issue.

Applying material from Item C and your knowledge of research methods, evaluate the strengths and limitations of using self-completion questionnaires to investigate the impact of pupil subcultures on educational achievement. (20 marks)

(e) Make sure you use the general L2 points outlined on pages 48–50 and try to apply the method to L2 and L3 issues in each paragraph. Remember to use the item and remember that the focus is on pupil subcultures. The first paragraph provides some information on types of subcultures and how they are formed and the second paragraph gives you strengths and a limitation of self-completion questionnaires. You could structure your answer around PET and use WWWE for your introduction as outlined in Template 1 (page 45).

(06) Outline and explain two arguments against the view that sociology can be value free. (10 marks)

(e) You are only required to give two arguments. Remember that these should be *against* the view that sociology can be (not 'should be') value free. You need to analyse the arguments and relate them to different perspectives such as interpretivism and postmodernism. As well as specific evaluation points, the two arguments presented can be evaluated through a comparison with the positivist view.

Student A

01 ■ Language. The working class may have a restricted language code, which means they are less able to succeed in subjects like English.

■ Parental aspirations. If working-class parents take less interest in their child's education the children are less likely to want to succeed in school.

ⓔ 4/4 marks awarded. Two appropriate factors are explained.

02 ■ Sure Start. This introduced a range of provisions such as nursery places and parenting classes for the working class, which were aimed at helping to raise achievement.

■ Education Action Zones. These provided extra resources in deprived areas in order to improve the quality of education in schools mainly attended by working-class pupils.

■ Pupil premium. This is when schools are given additional funding to support disadvantaged, usually working-class, students (e.g. those in care or on free school meals) through various interventions such as extra lessons or trips.

ⓔ 6/6 marks awarded. Three appropriate policies are explained.

03 There are various internal and external reasons for gender differences in achievement as outlined in Item A. An internal reason is the 'feminisation' of education. It has been argued by Sewell (2006) that schools do not celebrate qualities such as competitiveness and leadership, which are seen as more masculine traits. Many primary schools have non-competitive sports days which may put boys off school. On the other hand, female traits such as being well organised and being more attentive in lessons are rewarded. The feminisation of education can be illustrated by the introduction of coursework, which favours girls as they take better care of their work and are more likely to meet deadlines. Gorard argued that the main reason why the 'gender gap' in achievement in GCSEs referred to in Item A developed in the 1980s was that it coincided with the introduction of coursework. This relates to the issue of 'differences in attitude and application' mentioned in the item as research suggests that girls are better organised and can concentrate for longer periods than boys. This has meant that boys are more likely to do better in exams as they would cram revision in at the last minute. However, as Elwood (2005) argues, exams have a bigger influence on final grades. Also the recent reduction in coursework and the fact that it now usually takes place in school as 'controlled assessments' means that girls' being more organised, meeting deadlines etc. will give them less of an advantage.

🄔 The candidate has successfully applied the reference to 'differences in attitude and application' and achievement in GCSEs. It is a good technique to directly quote what point is being applied from the item.

A second reason why girls may be achieving more than boys is the external factor of changes in women's employment that can be seen to be the result of the 'impact of feminism' as stated in the item. Since 1975, the pay gap between men and women has fallen due to the Equal Pay Act. The Sex Discrimination Act has meant that women are more protected in the workplace and so have better career opportunities. This legislation has meant that females now feel more able to break through the 'glass ceiling' and gain higher-status jobs. This has acted as an incentive for girls to work hard and achieve in school as they will see the possibility of a well-paid job at the end of their studies. Women are less likely to see themselves as being housewives and, as stated in Item A, are now more likely to go on to higher education than males, gaining more qualifications as a result. There is, however, continued inequality in women's employment. Despite the Equal Pay Act, recent figures suggest that the gender pay gap still exists and is actually increasing. Research by the World Economic Forum (2014) reported that the UK was ranked 1st out of 136 countries in terms of females entering into university and further education. However, the UK was ranked only 64th in terms of equality in estimated earned income. Changes in women's employment have therefore not increased in line with female improvements in education. This would suggest that the external factor of women's improved employment opportunities is not as important a factor in explaining gender differences in achievement as the feminisation of education.

🄔 **10/10 marks awarded.** For both reasons the candidate has successfully applied points from the item. In the second paragraph the impact of feminism and increased participation of women in higher education have both been applied and developed. Both reasons have been well analysed and have been appropriately evaluated with contemporary evidence.

04 As Item B states, certain groups such as black pupils and some Asians perform relatively poorly in education. The reasons for this are complex as demonstrated by the fact that some Asian groups, namely Indian, perform better than white students. Interactionists would argue that the reason why certain ethnic minority groups underachieve is down to internal factors such as negative teacher labelling and pupils' responses to this. However, functionalists would focus on external factors such as cultural deprivation when looking at the cause of differential ethnic achievement. They would argue that positive parental support and values are more important than any issues that occur in school.

🄔 This is a good introduction, which follows the AAA approach as outlined in Template 2.

In terms of racist labelling, Wright (1992) found that Asian students were often the victim of negative treatment from teachers. Teachers assumed that they would have a poor grasp of English and would tend to misspell and mispronounce their names. This would lower their self-esteem and cause them to underachieve. Gillborn and Youdell (2000) found that teachers already had 'racialised expectations' towards black pupils and would see their behaviour as a threat. As a result black students felt they were being picked on and would underachieve. It could be argued that the reason why black Caribbean pupils are more likely to be excluded, as referred to in Item B, is because of these 'racialised expectations'. If teachers treat them unfairly and see them as a 'threat' they would be more likely to get excluded and they will miss out on school and therefore underachieve as a result. However, functionalists would argue that the more likely reason for this statistic is that black students are often culturally deprived due to inadequate socialisation. For example, values such as immediate gratification are passed on where black parents would encourage their children to leave school as soon as possible and not teach the value of education. Similarly, New Right thinker Murray would argue that black pupils are more likely to be part of an underclass with female-headed families and the resulting lack of a male role model. However, interactionists such as Keddie would reject the cultural deprivation approach as 'victim blaming' and would argue that internal school-based factors such as streaming are more important.

e A good coverage of labelling, which is well evaluated with use of the functionalist perspective. This criticism from Keddie is well applied to internal factors.

Even if negatively labelled by teachers, ethnic minority students can still achieve. As Fuller's study on black girls illustrates, students who want to succeed can reject teacher labels and get together to form a pro-education subculture. However, Mirza's study shows that attempts to do this and reject help from teachers they see as racist may not be successful for some black female students. Sewell (1998) found that black boys fell into four types of response to the racist stereotype that they felt teachers had of them as being 'trouble'. While the 'rebels' rejected goals and rules of school and were likely to underachieve, they were only the minority. The largest group were the 'conformists' who accepted school and goals and wanted to achieve despite this labelling. While Sewell's study may be out of date, it has the strength of illustrating how pupils can respond to labelling in different ways. He also accepts that factors outside of school such as a lack of a male role model and the media can influence the achievement of black boys.

(e) Three accounts of student responses to labelling are analysed with some good evaluation of Sewell.

> Marxists and Weberians, however, would argue that by focusing on internal factors interactionists are ignoring material factors and the impact of racism in wider society. It can be argued that some ethnic minorities such as Bangladeshi and Pakistani suffer from material deprivation due to racial discrimination in the labour market. This means that due to a low family income they may lack access to materials such as educational equipment and a quiet place to study and so may underachieve as a result. Noon's study provides evidence that there is racial discrimination in areas such as employment, which may have a knock-on effect on educational achievement. If students from an ethnic minority background feel that employers are racist this may act as a disincentive to work hard to get qualifications in school. This may be more of an important factor on whether they achieve than any negative labelling by teachers, who are unlikely to be overtly racist in a school through fear of losing their job.

(e) External factors of material deprivation and racism in wider society are presented, linked to achievement and applied well to internal factors at the beginning and end of the paragraph.

> Rather than the negative labelling of individual teachers, another internal factor that may influence ethnic minorities' achievement is that schools as a whole are institutionally racist. It has been argued by Coard that UK schools are ethnocentric, meaning that education favours British white culture and therefore giving priority to white pupils who are therefore more likely to achieve. An ethnocentric curriculum may produce underachievement for groups such as black students in subjects like history. For example, if the image of black people is portrayed negatively in lessons on slavery then this may damage black students' self-esteem and can lead to failure in a subject like history. However, the ethnocentric curriculum cannot be the only cause of the ethnic gap in underachievement as Chinese pupils achieve highest despite the curriculum being biased against their culture. Sociologists who look at external factors would argue that the high achievement of Chinese pupils is more due to the importance that is placed on getting a good education at home by so-called 'tiger mums'.

(e) The candidate has differentiated types of internal factors and has evaluated the potential impact of an ethnocentric curriculum by referring to different ethnic groups. There is another good attempt to assess the relative importance of internal with external factors.

Government policies that have introduced greater selection by schools, such as parentocracy, have led to another internal factor which is likely to disadvantage students from ethnic minority backgrounds. Evidence suggests that schools can be racist in their admission policies such as using primary school reports to avoid selecting certain ethnic groups. It also may be more difficult for parents from some ethnic backgrounds to get their child into a 'good' school as they may lack the cultural capital required such as knowledge of admissions procedures. This may apply to students whose parents do not have English as their first language. While Marxist-influenced sociologists would argue that the selection system is biased towards white, middle-class parents, functionalists argue that the system offers equal opportunities. They would argue that if ethnic minority parents miss out on their choice of school it is more likely to be caused by cultural deprivation as they are probably not doing enough to get their child into a good school.

e Another internal factor is well presented, and analysed. While there is no reference to a specific ethnic group, the candidate does apply language issues to the selection process. There is another attempt at evaluation at the end, with the functionalist view on this issue.

Perhaps the main reason why there is an ethnic gap in achievement is due to the internal factor of teacher labelling. However, this may not be applicable to all ethnic groups, such as the Chinese and Indians, who outperform white students.

e This is a very brief conclusion, largely a repeat of the point made in the introduction. The candidate does not explain why labelling is felt to be the most important factor.

e **27/30 marks awarded.** Overall a wide range of internal and external factors on different reasons for differential achievement of ethnic minorities are presented, explained and evaluated. Outside school factors are applied well to internal factors rather than being presented by juxtaposition. The essay is conceptually detailed and a range of different ethnic groups are referred to. The candidate does not, however, make use of the item in terms of the interplay between class, gender and ethnicity. The conclusion adds little and does not follow the suggestions as outlined in Template 2.

05 A self-completion questionnaire is a list of standardised questions, usually closed, with pre-coded answers which the respondent fills out on their own. They are used by positivists as they are reliable and produce large amounts of quantitative data. However, interpretivists reject their use as the data gained lacks validity. In the case of investigating the importance of subcultures on achievement, they would argue that unstructured interviews would be a better method to gain verstehen on issues such as how students who belong to an anti-school subculture have different values to the school and fail as a result.

ⓔ This is a clear introduction following the WWWE outlined in Template 1 and there is an attempt at L3 in the last sentence.

The first practical problem a researcher will have is gaining access to the school from gatekeepers such as the head teacher and gaining informed consent from parents. With a self-completion questionnaire, however, there is no contact between the researcher and respondents so the head teacher may be willing to have the researcher email questionnaires to staff and students or give them out to students to fill out in a tutor period. This way the researcher will not need to spend time and money getting a CRB check. As the item states, pupils are used to filling out questionnaires in school so there may be a high response rate. However, the topic is potentially a sensitive one and a head teacher may not want a researcher publishing results about the negative attitudes of students who belong to an anti-school subculture. If the results show that there are a large number of students in anti-school subcultures who are not interested in achievement (such as they do not do homework) this will reflect negatively on the image of the school.

ⓔ There are some good L2 points on access, which have been developed and applied well to the method. A good attempt at L3 at the end is linked to access although it is not applied to the method.

Practical advantages will be cost and time. Once access is gained it would be very easy to distribute questionnaires to the whole school population at a low cost. By having tick-box questions the researcher could easily spot trends between different ethnic groups and whether students feel that they belong to a subculture, whether it is pro- or anti-school and whether it has a positive or negative effect on their achievement. This would lead to the theoretical advantage, useful for positivists, of being able to look for correlations between variables such as ethnicity and gender and belonging to different subcultures. As they are self-completion, the researcher could use postal questionnaires or email to send to different geographical areas. This would allow comparisons to be made on whether anti-school subcultures are more likely to exist in inner-city schools or rural areas.

ⓔ There are two attempts at L3 as the candidate has applied characteristics of the method to the topic. However, with the second there is no reference to achievement.

> As Item C mentions, a problem with self-completion questionnaires is that as there is no researcher present so there may be issues with respondents completing them. Even though they only have to tick a box, students with literacy issues, who are more likely to be in bottom sets and part of an anti-school culture, may find it difficult to read the questions. It is also likely that these students may simply not want to fill in a questionnaire to do with school, particularly if it is about why they are underachieving. On the other hand, those in a pro-school culture may be more willing to respond and fill in questions that ask about how their peer group is a positive influence and helps them achieve, e.g. do you belong a study group? The issue that the sample may lack representativeness could also apply to parents. While, as the item states, questionnaires could be passed on to parents by students, it is more likely that parents from a working-class background are less likely to fill them in as they stereotypically value education less than middle-class parents. There is also the problem that some students, particularity those in an anti-school subculture, do not pass the questionnaire on to their parents.

ⓔ There are two good L3 points here, which are clearly applied to the method by phrases such as 'filling in' and 'ticking boxes'. There is a good L2 developed from the item about parents but this is not related to subcultures or achievement.

> A main benefit of self-completion questionnaires is that there are few ethical issues and anonymity can be guaranteed. This could lead to the theoretical strength of increased validity in responses. However, students may see the researcher who asks them to complete the questionnaire in a tutor period as a 'teacher in disguise'. Those in an anti-school subculture may not want to respond honestly to a question about whether their peer group truants and encourages them not to do homework as they will be worried that they might get into trouble. Similarly, teachers may see the researcher as 'Ofsted in disguise' and may not want to be seen as a bad teacher. If they tick a box stating that students in their lessons are part of an anti-school culture and that they cannot control their behaviour and they are failing, as they might be afraid that their job would be under threat.

ⓔ There are two developed L3s in this paragraph, which are related to anonymity, validity and the characteristics of pupils and teachers.

> While self-completion questionnaires can be potentially useful for gathering basic information on whether subcultures exist in a school, their main weakness is the theoretical issue that they lack validity. The topic of subcultures is a complex issue and interpretivists would argue that it is unlikely that questionnaires would uncover the meanings behind how belonging to a subculture can affect achievement.

ⓔ This is a reasonable conclusion, which identifies a main weakness of the method.

ⓔ **20/20 marks awarded.** Overall there are a range of L2 and L3 points in each paragraph. Most of the L3s are developed with use of PET and examples of the types of issues that could be raised by investigating the topic with self-complete questionnaires. While the response mainly focuses on pupils, there are good references to potential issues of using the method with teachers and parents.

---

06 Positivists argue that by using methods such as official statistics and questionnaires, sociology can be value free as the researcher is able to not let their own beliefs get in the way of conducting their research. While sociology cannot be as objective as the natural sciences, it can still try to be objective when using methods to study cause and effect. This view is rejected by Weber who argues that rather than being value free, sociologists are value laden during certain stages of the research process. When choosing a topic, for example, so-called scientific sociologists such as Durkheim are inevitably going to be influenced by their values. Weber would argue that Durkheim made a subjective decision to study the topic of suicide as a result of one of his relatives taking his own life. Weber does, however, feel that sociologists can be value free when they are conducting their research. However, when they interpret their data and make recommendations from their findings, Weber argues that sociologists are once again inevitably going to be influenced by their own beliefs and therefore cannot be value free.

Critical sociologists such as Marxists would also reject the notion of a value-free sociology. They would argue that research topics are chosen with the aim of challenging the inequalities that exist in society. Socialist Peter Townsend chose to conduct his survey on poverty as he wanted to draw attention to his claim that the government was not doing enough to eradicate poverty. Gouldner would argue that sociologists have a moral responsibility to draw attention to such issues in their research and he would argue that value freedom in sociology is neither possible nor desirable. He would argue that sociologists should be 'value committed' rather than value free.

ⓔ **8/10 marks awarded.** The candidate has a good knowledge and understanding of two reasons. There is appropriate application and analysis of some examples but more points needed to be developed to achieve a maximum mark. For example, in the first paragraph the criticism by Weber could have been linked to the interpretivist approach and methods that are subjective rather than objective. In paragraph two, examples of issues that sociologists have a 'moral responsibility' to bring into the public domain could have been discussed.

Total score: 75/80 marks = a top grade A

Student B

01 Poor parental attitudes and lack of intellectual development.

ⓔ **2/4 marks awarded.** Two appropriate factors are identified but neither is explained.

02 Mixed-ability classes within schools may have had an impact on how those from the working class achieved in schools. If there are no streams then different classes can work together meaning that working-class pupils can have a chance to work with brighter pupils who may help them progress. Another factor that could have contributed to social class differences would have been the opposite of the above: streaming. This would possibly have had a negative effect on working-class pupils, as some studies suggest that they would have been placed in the bottom set groups within school, and would be behind other groups in their work. A third factor that could have contributed to social class differences could be vocational education, which could offer opportunities to those better suited to practical, work-based learning. Working-class pupils might find them more interesting than academic studies. A fourth factor is the raising of the school leaving age. This is more likely to help the working class achieve as they were more likely to leave school at 16. Now they have to carry on in education to get a C in maths and English.

ⓔ **4/6 marks awarded.** The first two points on mixed ability and streaming refer to policies that might be adopted by individual schools rather than a government policy so they do not score. Both vocational education and the raising of the school leaving age are explained and therefore score marks. If you are able and have time, a good strategy is to give an extra point. As has happened in this response, you may gain extra marks for the additional response. For small-mark questions you will save time by using bullet points for answers. This response is unnecessarily detailed; for example, there is no need to write out the question, which the candidate has repeated several times.

03 Feminism has led to a large impact on gender differences in achievement as feminists have argued that there needs to be greater gender equality. Many factors from outside of the education system may have inspired this change. First, feminism has become popular during the last few decades, where women have been arguing for equal rights. Feminists argue that women are seen only as sex objects who are only around to benefit men. They believe that they have been treated unfairly by men, and that they should have equal rights in society. Within the education system, girls have started to be included in practical subjects, such as science and technology, whereas, before, they would have been only allowed to do home economics, which involved sewing and cooking and learning how to be a good wife. This would have been a factor for girls receiving an opportunity to work within the same subjects as boys, as many women would have protested and argued for change. Although not as much as before, some subjects are still seen as 'boys' subjects and some are 'girls' subjects. Boys in particular might not choose a subject due to peer pressure from a laddish subculture that they belong to. However, it could be argued that this is less common today as boys may be less likely to be afraid of bullying from doing dance because of street dance groups like 'Diversity' making it more acceptable. As a result of girls being able to do the same subjects as boys, their achievement may have improved as they can now choose subjects they are interested in and so achieve more.

e **4/10 marks awarded.** The candidate identifies one factor, the impact of feminism. However, for the most part the discussion is focused on subject choice and more general points about feminist views. While issues to do with greater subject choice could have been used to explain improved achievement, this has only been done briefly in the last sentence.

04 Sociologists argue that there are differences between ethnic groups towards education such as Chinese and Indian pupils performing better on average in GCSE than white, Bangladeshi and black pupils. There are a wide range of different sociological explanations for this that are based on different evidence and concepts.

e This introduction offers little and is largely a recycling of the item.

It can be argued that a main reason why different ethnic groups achieve differently is down to material deprivation. This refers to a lack of things that money can buy which can be used to help with school. Studies show that Pakistani and Bangladeshi students are three times more likely to be poor than white students because of things such as racist employers. As a result of a lack of money they are more likely to live in overcrowded homes, resulting in no space to study and excessive distraction from other family members and therefore fail.

e This section does try to explain why certain ethnic minorities experience material deprivation and how this can cause underachievement but it has not been applied to the question and linked to internal factors.

Other sociologists argue that black and white working-class homes lack the correct values to achieve such as fatalism. This means that they don't feel like they can do anything about their future and therefore see little point in working hard at school. Some sociologists argue that language plays an important role in achievement. Some Asian and Polish students may suffer as they cannot express themselves verbally or write in good English. Some Afro-Caribbean students may talk in a dialect which can mean that they will be at a disadvantage in terms of their communication skills. However, the Swann Report states that by the age of 16 most students whose first language is not English have caught up. Also schools do a lot to give extra support for students if they can't speak English well.

e A fair account of cultural deprivation and some good evaluation but again the material has not been applied as an alternative to internal factors.

> However, a weakness of these outside school factors is that they generalise about ethnic groups and don't take account of the diverse nature of ethnicity in the UK. Some of these arguments can also be described as blaming the victim as they suggest that ethnic underachievement occurs as a result of cultural deprivation. Keddie argues that just like the working class, ethnic minorities cannot be deprived of their own culture. They are culturally different not inferior. The real cause of underachievement is the school system which penalises ethnic minorities for not having the 'correct' white middle-class values.

e While this paragraph has an evaluative stance, it is only specifically applied to internal factors in the last sentence.

> As a result of these criticisms interactionist sociologists have looked at internal factors such as teacher labelling. Wright found that black students were typically stereotyped as 'disruptive and lazy' by teachers and subsequently placed in lower sets and exam tiers. A negative self-fulfilling prophecy would develop as a result, as black students would live up to this label and then form anti-school subcultures and therefore they would fail.

e This paragraph links the material above on external factors to the question. However, this is done by juxtaposition — a better strategy would have been to do this from the outset.

> Another in-school factor is the ethnocentric curriculum which only focuses on one cultural perspective and ignores others. Ethnic groups such as Bangladeshi and Chinese students can develop low self-esteem as a result of only studying English culture. However, it could be argued that the National Curriculum is very multicultural and that a wide variety of different cultures are studied. For example, in Year 9 RE lessons students learn about Islam and in English they study poetry from across the world as well as Shakespeare. Also institutional racism occurs as black and Asian pupils have historically been put into lower sets, due to them having a different accent or speaking a different language. As teachers give less support to pupils in lower sets they are more likely to underachieve. Evidence also suggests that schools have been institutionally racist as they haven't dealt with racist issues in schools. However, this is less true today as racist incidents are dealt with effectively and have to be reported to the local authority.

e There is a good coverage of more internal factors here, which have been well evaluated.

While internal factors such as racist teacher labelling are important, evidence suggests that pupils can respond to labelling in different ways. As Fuller's study shows, labels can be rejected and mean that students from ethnic minority backgrounds (in this case black girls) can work hard to prove them wrong and achieve as a result.

External factors such as parental values and support clearly have a key role as well and may help to explain why Chinese students are the highest achievers. Another external factor is a lack of material support which may help to explain why groups such as Bangladeshi students underachieve as they are more likely to be poorer than most other ethnic groups.

Finally, as the item suggests, factors other than ethnicity can influence achievement such as gender and class. For example, black females achieve much higher than black males and white working-class male students are one of the lowest achieving groups.

e This is a good conclusion in terms of identifying different ethnic groups and relating them to different sociological explanations. There is also a good application of the item to the issue of gender which is developed with 'something new' on class. Some of these could have gone in the main body of the essay and have been developed.

e **19/30 marks awarded.** Overall this has a good range of knowledge on sociological explanations of both internal and external causes of differences in ethnicity achievement. There is some good evaluation in the paragraphs on internal factors and in the conclusion. However, it would have been better to start the essay with internal factors as this is the focus of the question. External factors should then have been clearly applied to internal factors in the form of evaluation. There is also a lack of depth of material on pupil responses to labelling and subcultures.

05 Self-completion questionnaires would be a good method to use in order to investigate subcultures. As the item suggests, they would be useful as they can be completed anonymously. This method is preferred by positivists as it achieves their main goals of reliability, representativeness and generalisability. As the questions are standardised, the method is reliable. This means that the method could be easily replicated. As the data gathered is quantitative it can be used to look at correlations and test a hypothesis.

e The first part of the introduction offers little, but the candidate demonstrates some reasonable knowledge on the method.

> A practical strength of self-completion questionnaires is that they are relatively cheap and easy to produce since there is no need to recruit and train interviewers as you would need to do for group interviews. The method would therefore be attractive to researchers who have little funding. Another practical strength is that once you have gained access to the school you have a ready-made sample that is stratified by age. This would make it easy to see whether, as Woods suggests, there are different adaptations by students. For example, results from the questionnaire from Year 7 students could be compared with Year 11 to test the hypothesis that anti-school subculture increase as students get older.

e This paragraph has some good L1 material on practical issues, which is developed with an example and comparison with interviews. There is a well-developed L2 but this is not related to achievement.

> With questionnaires there may be the problem of a low response rate. For example, those in an anti-school subculture are less likely to complete as only those with a strong interest in the subject are likely to fill in. This means that the sociologists may not be able to generalise from the data as the sample is no longer representative of the cross section of the students in the school.

e There is an attempt at L3 here with a good point on subculture but it lacks explanation and is not applied to achievement.

> Some respondents may not take the questionnaire seriously and may lie and give socially desirable answers. This will mean that the data will lack validity. Interpretivists would also reject them because questionnaires are the most detached of all methods as there is no contact between the researcher and the respondent. Unless the researcher is allowed in the classroom when they give the questionnaires out they also will not know who filled them in.

e Some good theoretical problems are raised but these are not applied. There is a brief L2 with the reference to classrooms but this is not developed.

> In conclusion, while positivists favour questionnaires, interpretivists would argue that they lack validity so they would rather use other methods to investigate subcultures. A better way would be to use unstructured interviews but this is even more difficult to get permission to do in a school as it would take up more lesson time for students to complete.

ⓔ The first sentence of the conclusion adds little as it is largely a repeat. There is a hint at L2 in the last sentence regarding access issues.

ⓔ **15/20 marks awarded.** Overall this response shows a fair knowledge of the method but there are only limited attempts at application. There is one reasonable L2 point in the second paragraph but the other three L2s are only stated. There is one attempt at L3 but this is not linked to achievement.

> **06** Some sociologists argue that sociologists can be scientific and objective when conducting research. However, interpretivists argue that human behaviour cannot be studied objectively and that sociologists cannot be value free. They argue that the main aim of sociology should be to uncover the meanings that individual actors have for their behaviour. As Weber argues, the way to do this is gain verstehen through using more qualitative methods such as participant observation and unstructured interviews. As both these methods mean that sociologists cannot be detached from the people being studied, value freedom is impossible. For example, when using interviews it may be difficult for the interviewer not to influence respondents due to interviewer bias that occurs in the interaction process during the interview. Similarly with participant observation the researcher may 'go native' which can mean that they may become biased towards the group being studied. Foote Whyte stated that he changed from being a participant observer to a non-observing participant. He got too carried away with joining in with the activities of the group being studied, such as playing baseball, and therefore became subjective and was no longer value free.

ⓔ **5/10 marks awarded.** This response has demonstrated some reasonable knowledge and understanding of one reason, namely the interpretivist view that it is impossible to study human behaviour objectively. If you are asked for two reasons, you will not be able to gain more than half marks if you only offer one. There is some analysis of the interpretivist criticism that research has to be subjective, with examples of research methods, and one is developed with the use of a study.

Total score: 49/80 marks = a high grade C

■Test paper 4

AS Paper 1

(01) Define the term 'hidden curriculum'.   (2 marks)

ⓔ It is a good idea to give an example, such as 'being on time for lessons', with your definition. If your definition is incorrect the example may score 1 mark.

(02) Using one example, briefly explain how gender socialisation may affect subject choice.   (2 marks)

ⓔ Here you can refer to gender socialisation either at home or at school. For example, gender-stereotypical toys bought by parents could lead to differences in subject choice, such as construction toys encouraging boys to take up science and technical subjects. In terms of school, gendered subject images such as teachers presenting science as a 'male subject' could be related to girls' low take-up of science subjects. If you have time, you could give a second example.

(03) Outline three ways in which some sociologists have criticised the functionalist view of the role of education.   (6 marks)

ⓔ As well as specific criticisms of the functionalist view of the role of education, such as the existence of unemployed graduates contradicting the notion of meritocracy, you could base your responses on different theoretical criticisms (see page 7). Again, time permitting; you could give an additional criticism.

(04) Outline and explain two ways in which cultural factors may lead to the underachievement of pupils from some ethnic minority groups.   (10 marks)

ⓔ Make sure that you are giving 'cultural' rather than 'material' factors. Do not make the mistake of listing factors as you only need to look at two but in some depth. You will be rewarded not only for applying points clearly to the underachievement of specific ethnic groups, but also for brief evaluation, such as referring to the relative importance of material or internal factors.

(05) Read Item A below and answer the question that follows.

> **Item A**
>
> Since the 1980s successive governments have implemented a range of policies aimed at introducing market forces into the state education system. It is claimed that marketisation policies, such as league tables and increasing diversity in the types of schools that parents can choose to send their children to, would increase competition and so raise standards. However, some sociologists have been critical of such policies and have argued that the education market favours middle-class parents.

Applying material from Item A and your own knowledge, evaluate the claim that marketisation policies in education have increased inequality between social classes.   (20 marks)

Questions & Answers

e Make sure that you always read the question very carefully — note that this is talking about increased INequality. You could use the AAA approach as outlined in Template 2 for item-based essays as this will ensure your introduction applies the item (use the first paragraph to help define marketisation) and gets off to an evaluative start. As well as polices of the Conservative government, such as those in the 1988 ERA, you should refer to polices introduced by New Labour and the Coalition government of 2010–15 such as different types of academies. These policies should be related to the New Right view that, as stated in Item A, standards would increase for all social classes, therefore rejecting the essay claim. Arguments to support the essay claim would come from the Marxist perspective and evidence from sociologists such as Ball and Gerwitz which criticises policies such as parentocracy as benefiting the middle class (see page 10).

(06) Read Item B below and answer the question that follows.

> ## Item B
>
> ### Investigating the impact of teacher labelling on achievement
>
> Many sociologists are interested in the ways in which teacher–pupil interaction in the classroom can affect achievement. Negative teacher labelling has been found to have a negative impact on pupils' self-image and lead to a self-fulfilling prophecy of failure. This type of labelling may also result in certain students being placed in lower sets. Research also suggests that pupils can respond to teacher labelling in a variety of ways such as developing both pro- and anti-school subcultures.
>
> By using participant observation to study labelling, sociologists are able to see for themselves how teachers may label and how different groups of students react to these labels. However, as well as ethical problems, particularly with covert observation, the researcher has the issue of what role they should adopt within the school while conducting their research.

Applying material from Item B and your knowledge of research methods, evaluate the strengths and limitations of using participant observation to investigate the impact of teacher labelling on educational achievement. (20 marks)

e In your introduction you could use WWWE as outlined in Template 1 to ensure you locate the method in a theoretical context. Make sure you use the general L2 points outlined on pages 48–50. A good place to start would be with access into school as this is one the first practical issues a sociologist would have to consider when conducting primary research in a school. The second paragraph of the item gives you a strength and limitations of participant observation, so make sure you use them. Try to apply these clearly to the topic of the role of teacher labelling on achievement. You will get some ideas on how to do this from the first paragraph, such as being placed in lower sets, but remember not to just copy from the item. Labelling by teachers could occur in relation to gender, class and ethnic achievement, so use these to develop L3 points. For example, teachers will not want to appear to be racist or sexist and have a negative impact on achievement in front of a researcher who they may see as 'Ofsted in disguise'. You could structure your answer around PET but make sure that you apply the method to L2 and L3 issues in each paragraph.

AS Paper 2 (Section A)

(01) Outline two problems of using unstructured interviews in sociological research. (4 marks)

ⓔ Make sure that you refer to problems of unstructured rather than structured interviews. If you have time, you could give a third problem.

(02) Evaluate the advantages of using documents in sociological research. (16 marks)

ⓔ Use Template 1 for methods questions and you should refer to the specific advantages of personal, public and historical documents. Make sure you focus on advantages and only refer to disadvantages if they are tied into strengths. You could refer to Scott's four criteria when evaluating the relative advantages of different types of documents (see the comment on page 40).

A-level Paper 1

(01) Outline two ways in which globalisation has influenced educational policies. (4 marks)

ⓔ You could refer to policies that have been introduced in response to the changes in the economy brought about by globalisation. In addition to government policies such as on EAL funding and New Labour's emphasis on 'lifelong learning', you could refer to policies that individual schools may have adopted such as American-based behaviour management programmes adopted by some academies.

(02) Outline three ways in which factors inside the education system may have contributed to the improvement in girls' achievement. (6 marks)

ⓔ To gain full marks you must explain how each factor may have improved girls' achievement. Make sure that you refer to internal and not external factors. If you have time, you could give a fourth factor.

(03) Read Item A below and answer the question that follows.

> **Item A**
>
> Some sociologists argue that a major role of the education system is that it should provide equal opportunities for all pupils to succeed so that they can be allocated to their most appropriate role in the economy. However, statistics on achievement suggest that schools systematically fail the majority of working-class pupils. Sociologists critical of this view have put forward a number of reasons why working-class students end up in working-class jobs.

Applying material from Item A, analyse two ways in which the education system legitimates or reproduces social inequalities. (10 marks)

ⓔ You are only required to give two reasons and these *must* be applied from material in the item. The reference to the functionalist view of equal opportunities and role allocation in Item A could be applied to the Marxist view of Bowles and Gintis of the 'myth of meritocracy' and its role in legitimating inequality. The reference in the item to 'statistics' could be applied to the examination system, which is seen by functionalists as illustrating how the education system is meritocratic due to its standardised nature. Triggers from the item that could be applied to reproduction of social inequalities are the references to the working class systematically failing and how working-class students get working-class jobs. These could be analysed by reference to Willis' lads, Althusser or Bourdieu's theory of cultural reproduction. The reasons given should be analysed in some depth but evaluation will also be rewarded. An introduction is not required and a conclusion, if you write one, should be brief.

(04) Read Item B below and answer the question that follows.

Item B

Research suggests that social class, gender and ethnicity can all significantly influence educational achievement. Some sociologists argue that differences in achievement are due to factors that take place in the home.

For example, evidence suggests that family structure and levels of parental interest in education are crucial to a child's development. Linguistic skills that children have when they start school can vary significantly between different social groups. The amount of financial resources a family has can also have a major positive or negative effect on educational success.

Applying material from Item B and your own knowledge, evaluate the view that home factors are the main cause of differences in the educational achievement of different social groups.   (30 marks)

📝 Remember to use Template 2 for item-based essays. As Item B suggests, you should refer to class, gender and ethnic-based differences in achievement. As well as specific evaluation of home factors, you should use internal factors to evaluate the importance of factors at home on differences in achievement in the three social groups. Aim to refer to a variety of different home factors, both material and cultural, as stated in the item, and clearly link the factors discussed to the achievement of the three different groups. Consider the relative importance of different home factors and internal factors in relation to all groups, as well as the interplay between class, gender and ethnicity on achievement.

(05) Read Item C below and answer the question that follows.

Item C

Investigating differences in gender achievement and subject choice

There has been growing concern since the 1980s over the increasing 'gender gap' in achievement. As well as knowing the nature and extent of patterns of gender achievement, sociologists have examined various changes both in society and in school that may account for these differences. Sociologists have also been interested in patterns of subject choice and why it is that certain subjects are chosen more by girls than boys.

Sociologists may use official statistics to study differences in gender achievement and subject choice. The government collects educational statistics from every school in the country. Statistics on both subject choice and achievement could be used to examine the impact of educational policies in these areas. However, while official statistics may show patterns in gender achievement and subject choice, they do not offer an explanation as to why they occur.

Applying material from Item C and your knowledge of research methods, evaluate the strengths and limitations of using official statistics to investigate differences in gender achievement and subject choice. (20 marks)

ⓔ In your introduction you could use WWWE as outlined in Template 1 and structure your answer around PET. Make sure you use the general L2 points outlined on pages 48–50 and try to apply the method to L2 and L3 issues in each paragraph. Remember to use the item and note that the focus is on differences in both gender achievement and subject choice. The first paragraph in Item C provides some information on this and has a trigger to official statistics with the reference to 'patterns'. The second paragraph gives you strengths and a limitation of official statistics and has the trigger of using them to study the effectiveness of policies (such as GIST) that could be used for an L3 application point.

(06) **Outline and explain two advantages of using field experiments in sociological research.** (10 marks)

ⓔ You are only required to give two advantages. Remember that these should be related to field not laboratory experiments. Analyse the advantages through the use of studies and locate them within a theoretical context. You should categorise the advantages by use of PET and could tie in disadvantages in order to develop evaluation.

Knowledge check answers

1 Possible answers include: providing specific skills such as IT; providing general skills such as team work; 'bridging' the gap between the family and the workplace; socialising pupils into values required in the economy such as punctuality; role allocation.

2 Possible answers include: knowledge of the arts such as Shakespeare and classical music; experiences such as visits to museums and art galleries; more expressive language; being socialised into manners that do not question authority; parents having a better knowledge of the education system and admissions procedures.

3 Possible answers include: creating a two-tier education system; the myth of parentocracy, as greater selection disadvantages males, working class and certain ethnic minority groups; middle-class parents having more cultural capital so that they are 'more skilled' choosers of school; Marxist criticisms that it reproduces inequality.

4 Possible answers include: there is still a National Curriculum that the majority of students follow; the majority of students follow the same types of assessment such as GCSE; there is a limited amount of vocational education; there is a lack of general preparation for diverse needs of the economy, for example business leaders have called for more 'soft' life skills to be taught in schools.

5 Possible answers include: poor diet and health; poor housing; lack of educational resources such as textbooks, calculators etc; unable to afford private tuition; unable to afford the costs of higher education; unable to afford to live in an area of a higher-achieving school.

6 Cultural deprivation argues that the working class lack the values needed for success in education whereas cultural capital argues that the middle class possess the values which enable them to achieve.

7 Possible answers include: pupils can reject teacher labels; sociologists such as functionalists argue that subcultural values develop from the poor values that working-class students bring into school; neo-Marxist Willis argues that subcultures develop as a result of working-class students rejecting the values of the school; teacher labelling can also result in students developing pro-school cultures.

8 Possible answers include:
   - *Black-Caribbean students:* lack of intellectual development; language dialect, being socialised into a subculture that does not value education, lack of a male role model (for boys); family structure being less resistant to racism.
   - *Asian students:* having English as a second language; the 'controlling' nature of family structure (particularly for girls).
   - *Eastern European and other immigrant groups:* having English as a second language.

For all groups you could refer to a lack of cultural capital, for example in relation to parental choice.

9 Possible answers include: the ethnocentric curriculum; schools having a low priority towards race-related issues such as dealing with racist incidents; ethnic minority groups being placed into lower sets due to issues such as language differences; Asian pupils, particularly girls, getting less attention from teachers; cultural traditions being ignored.

10 Possible answers include: toys bought by parents; games and activities parents and teachers encourage; gendered subject images; gender-stereotypical peer pressure; sex-typing of occupations.

11 Possible answers include: schools being allowed to opt out of local authority control and become academies; businesses and other groups being allowed to set up free schools; business sponsorship of schools; allowing educational services to be delivered by the private sector; formula funding; the PPPs initiative where private companies built state schools.

12 Possible answers include: simple random sampling; systematic random sampling; stratified random sampling.

13 Possible answers include: reliability as they can be replicated; can be used to establish correlations and test a hypothesis; allows a larger sample so the findings can be generalised; detachment means greater objectivity as there is no contact between the researcher and the respondent.

14 Possible answers include: deception; lack of informed consent; lack of right to withdraw for participants; researcher potentially taking part in immoral or illegal activities; potential harm to participants.

15 Possible answers include: not always easy to identify or control variables; not able to study the past; can only use small samples.

16 Hard official statistics are valid as they measure what they set out to measure, whereas soft official statistics may be socially constructed. For example, soft statistics can be manipulated or be based on the subjective opinion of those compiling them.

17 Possible answers include: they may be in the public domain so are quick and easy to obtain; cheap; they may be the only way of studying the past.

18 Possible answers include: participant observation; unstructured interviews; group interviews.

19 Verification is proving your own theory right whereas falsification is proving someone else's theory wrong.

20 Possible answers include: formula funding; exam league tables; opting out; open enrolment; business sponsorship of schools.

Note: Key terms are indicated by **bold** page numbers

Index

Index

Townsend, Peter 34
triangulation **29**
tuition fees 24, 25

U
unstructured interviews 34–35

V
validity 27
value consensus **7**
value freedom 42
verbal abuse 22

verstehen **28**
vocational education 9

W
Weber, Max 28, 42
Willis 8, 9, 14, 15, 22
Woods, on subculture 14
Wright, on labelling 17
WWWE (What, Who, Why and Evaluation) 32, 45

Y
Young and Willmott study 34